SEWN
HATS

SEWN HATS

Carla Hegeman Crim

WILEY

John Wiley & Sons, Inc.

Senior Editor
Roxane Cerda

Project Editor
Carol Pogoni

Editorial Manager
Christina Stambaugh

Vice President and Publisher
Cindy Kitchel

Vice President and Executive Publisher
Kathy Nebenhaus

Interior Design
Jennifer Mayberry

Cover Design
Jose Almaguer

Photography
Michelle Pemberton
redrocketphoto.com
Select photos, pages 107, 110, 116, and 159 by Carla Crim

Illustrations
Carla Hegeman Crim

Dedicated to my Grannies, Dolly Jane Barton and Cecilia Louise Hegeman. Thank you for not only allowing me, but encouraging me, to play with your yarn, buttons, and fabric. Your early inspiration (and crafty genes) are with me every day.

Acknowledgments

To Roxane Cerda, for first bringing me in to the world of Wiley Craft as a technical editor, then entrusting me with my own project. I thank you for providing guidance and resources in a manner that was always fun and motivating.

To Carol Pogoni, for your amazing editing skills, wit, and patience. Your incredible attention to detail is so very appreciated. Thank you for embracing my technical approach, and working your magic to make the words flow.

To our wonderful photographer, Michelle Pemberton, and all the models who showed off the fun, fashion, and functionality of such a wide range of hats.

To Julie Hummel and Emily Hinkle for keeping everything organized and on track.

To all the contributors for their diligence and creativity. It was an honor to collaborate with so many talented folks. I learned something new from each and every one of you.

To Jennifer Paganelli for your mentorship and unlimited supply of love and inspiration. Thank you for making me part of your beautiful world.

To Cathy Peckiconis, for your constant support. I so admire your cheerfulness, faith in God, and amazing brain. I can't even imagine being the Scientific Seamstress without you as my Head Technician.

To Tom Jordan, Marlo Troy, and Shannon Winters, for being there for me every day. You three and Cathy were my go-to advisors for everything from design ideas to writing style throughout this process. I am truly blessed to have you as friends and confidants.

To all those who helped bring my pattern company to life: testers, customers, and blog followers. It is your feedback that fuels me! It is an honor to share this sewing journey with you. I am continually amazed by your talent and passion for sewing.

To my good friends near and far, scientist and non-scientist, sewing and non-sewing . . . thanks for accepting and cheering me on, no matter what crazy tangent I took.

To my extended family, my little brother Blake, his sweet wife Sonja, and their adorable boys; my aunts, uncles, and cousins; my mother-in-law, Madge, and all of the Crim sisters, brothers, cousins, nieces, and nephews; and my stepkids Andy, Danny, and Emily, and my stepdaughter-in-law, Anna, thank you all for your love and encouragement.

To my parents, Louis and Elizabeth Hegeman, thank you for giving me a happy childhood and all the tools to make for a fulfilling adulthood. Thank you for pushing me academically when I so needed it, while still nurturing a sense of fun and creativity.

To my husband, Delmar, and our son, Louis, thanks for your help and patience during this year-long book-writing process. Thanks for trying on numerous hats, and stepping over explosions of fabrics and trims to deliver meals to me at the computer. You guys gave me the space I needed to work, but kept me grounded with your warmth and unconditional love.

The publisher would like to thank all of the patient and lovely models who contributed to this book, including Aaron, Addison, Amber, Brett, Brooke, Caden, Cormac, Elizabeth, Felicia, Fiona, Joe, Josh, Julie, Kate, Keira, Linda, Louis, Lynda, Lucas, Madison, MaryAnne, Max, Paul, Rowan, Ruby, Ryann, Sara, Sophie, Sydney, Sylvia, Tommy, and Tristan.

The Publisher also extends thanks to Lesley Jane for providing wardrobe support, www.lesleyjane.com.

Table of Contents

Introduction

The making of hats often brings to mind images of meticulous milliners and haute hatters working with specialized equipment and old-style forms. Professional hat makers had skills that could be attained only by years of training and practice, so finely made hats were quite costly and symbolic of wealth and status. Although you can find purveyors of expensive, handcrafted hats today, their types of toppers represent a very small proportion of the hats that are actually sold and worn in this day and age. Next time you are out and about, make note of the hats people are wearing. If it is spring or summer, you will see lots of sunhats, bucket hats, and other brimmed caps on people of all genders and ages. In colder weather, you will see folks bundled up in cozy fleece hats and faux fur–lined aviator caps. Most of these hats are mass-produced in factories using very basic sewing techniques and inexpensive materials.

A handmade sewn hat combines the finery of a traditional hat with the functionality of a modern, purchased hat. Hats, in fact, are one of the quickest and easiest accessory items to make at home. They do not require much in the way of materials, so you can produce something beautiful and one-of-a-kind without spending a lot of money. The techniques used to construct sewn hats are no different than those used to make quilts, garments, and handbags. Best of all, you can make something that is perfectly suited to the wearer in terms of color, style, and fit.

My own introduction to sewing hats came about when I was designing custom outfits for collector dolls. No little ensemble was complete without a matching hat or headdress. With such small models, I was able to experiment with lots of different styles and techniques. Once my son came along, I wanted to make hats for him, but didn't have the best luck with the patterns I tried. When I made the transition to patternmaking, I realized that fitting heads wasn't all that different than fitting bodies, and I was able to create all kinds of hats for my friends and family.

Hats make wonderful gifts for all ages. Soft little hats and precious bonnets are perfect for newborn babies. For toddlers, hats are essential for keeping heads warm and/or eyes shaded, depending on the season. Older children need hats for the same reason as toddlers, but they are much more amenable to wearing them if they are fun and imaginative. There is nothing like a box of cool hats to inspire creative play in children. Surprisingly, teens and tweens are big wearers of hats—the funkier the better! Adults appreciate hats that are both stylish and functional. Because hats are so easy to personalize with colors and embellishments, you can create something that is right up the recipient's alley. And I'm really hoping the fun ladies of the Red Hat Society will use this book to make amazing hats for one another.

For those who experience hair loss due to medical issues, a hat is not only a crowning glory, but also a great equalizer. In these situations, the presence of a comforting fabric warms the head and also allows for protection from the elements. Additionally, a stylish hat provides a sense of confidence for the hat wearer. Bad hair days or even no hair days are all equal under a hat!

Hats are a great way to breathe new life into your own wardrobe. A colorful hat gives a fun "pop" to basic casual wear. If you have a favorite coat, you can make a coordinating hat for an instant put-together look. And let's not forget dress-up time! From parties to plays, costumes to ceremonies, hats can completely set the mood. It is all the more perfect when you make the hat yourself.

This book contains instructions to make 35 different hats, each conceived by a talented designer who has a unique style and following in the sewing world. (You can find each designer's bio at the end of this book.) There are patterns for all skill levels. Because of the step-by-step instructions and detailed diagrams, even beginners should be able to construct the hats that are designated as intermediate–advanced. Chapter 1 outlines the tools, materials, and techniques you will need to get started. You can make each hat in a range of sizes and materials, so the design possibilities are endless. In addition, you will find an appendix full of embellishment options at the end of the book. Although some embellishments were designed with specific hats in mind, all of the embellishments will mix and match beautifully with other projects. So put on your thinking cap, because it is time to start sewing some hats!

1

MATERIALS, METHODS, SIZING, AND ILLUSTRATIONS GUIDE

This chapter outlines the basic supplies and simple skills needed to make any of the sturdy, great-fitting hats in this book. A list of sewing terminology is included here as well. Specific fabrics, interfacings, and notions are recommended within each individual pattern, but an overview of the different options available at sewing and craft-supply stores is also covered in this chapter. You can't make a well-fitting hat without first learning how to properly take head measurements, so check out the "Sizing" section at the end of this chapter for tips on selecting the right hat size and an explanation of how to take accurate head measurements. This book also includes pattern pieces for the hat patterns. All of the pattern pieces you need are conveniently located online at www.wiley.com/go/sewnhats. Simply navigate to the site, select the pattern you want, and print. Each pattern offers printing guidance, so you can select just the sizes you need and be sure your printouts will work. You can print each pattern as many times as you need, so no more tracing and no more trying to keep track of pattern sheets and pieces. (Note that a few patterns provide specific cutting measurements that are explained within the pattern directions, so those hats do not have pattern pieces.) By combining the right elements with your own artistic flair, you can create professional-looking, one-of-a-kind hats.

Tools and Techniques

You won't go mad getting geared up to make the hats in this book. I've listed the basic sewing tools you will need to complete the patterns in this book, but most of the needed supplies are standard sewing implements that you likely already have in your sewing basket. If not, you can readily find these items at any sewing or craft-supply store. If you are new to sewing, hat making is a great way to learn basic sewing terms and techniques that are used in garment and accessory making.

TOOLS

Basting tape This double-sided tape provides a strong temporary hold and is perfect for keeping folds in place during the stitching process. Permanent and wash-away varieties are available. For the projects in this book, I recommend Wash Away™ Wonder Tape. It has a very strong hold, and comes in a convenient ¼" width.

Bias tape In this book, *single fold bias tape* is used to cover seam allowances, and ***double fold bias tape*** is used to finish off band/brim seams. You can actually make bias tape by hand, but I generally purchase pre-cut and folded tape. Because the tape is on the inside of the hat, don't worry too much about color coordination. If you can't find a good match to the hat fabric, just go with a neutral-colored bias tape.

Glue stick The temporary holding power of a glue stick can make all the difference in slippery stitching situations. You can purchase glue sticks that are made especially for fabric, but I find all-purpose and school glue twist-tube sticks work just as well.

Hot glue gun & hot glue sticks Hot gluing is a quick way to permanently apply embellishments and trims. For best results, use a high-temperature gun and sticks.

Iron/Ironing board From fusing interfacing to putting finishing touches on a brim, you'll use an iron throughout the hat construction process. The word "press" shows up almost as many times as the word "stitch" in this book!

Liquid seam sealant To keep ribbons from unraveling, you can apply liquid seam sealant to the cut ends. It dries quickly and a small amount goes a long way to prevent fraying. Fray Check™ and Fray Block™ are two popular brands.

Marking pens/pencils For making dots or lines on light-colored fabrics, use a fine-tipped air- or water-soluble marker. For darker fabrics, use chalk or a light-colored fabric marking pencil. A variety of products are available to transfer more complex markings like embroidery designs. For example, you can sandwich dressmaker's carbon paper between the pattern and the fabric, and then transfer the design by tracing with a stylus or empty ballpoint pen. Another option is to trace the design (in reverse) onto a sheet of paper with a heat transfer pencil, then iron the markings on to the fabric.

Needles You should have an assortment of both hand and machine sewing needles on hand. For hand stitching, you will need small needles for finishing work and larger needles for projects that involve embroidery. Because you will be working with diverse weights and thicknesses of fabric, I recommend purchasing a variety pack of universal needles for your machine.

Pins Make sure you have an abundant supply of straight pins to hold pieces during the hat assembly process. *Quilting pins* are ideal because they are a nice length and their colorful heads are easy to spot and manipulate. You will also need safety pins (of various sizes) for inserting ribbons and elastic into casings.

Press cloth For some fabrics, you'll need to protect the material from the iron (and vice versa). Use lightweight cotton scraps or tea towels as a press cloth/barrier.

Rotary cutter, cutting mat, and ruler For several of the projects, dimensions rather than pattern pieces are provided. So, you will need to cut these pieces with a rotary cutter, self-healing mat, and a ruler. This method not only saves trees, but the rotary cutter also allows you to make extremely precise straight cuts in a fraction of the time it takes to do the job with scissors.

Scissors It is good to have a pair of large, sharp scissors for cutting out pattern pieces. Small, fine-tipped scissors are great for detail work like snipping seam allowances.

Seam ripper Essential for fixing boo-boos, the seam ripper is also great for precise stitch removal and making small cuts like buttonholes.

Sewing machine A basic model that does straight and zigzag stitches is all you need to sew even the fanciest of hats. When working in tight spots, it is helpful to remove the extension table so the arm is free.

Spray starch Great for getting out tough wrinkles, starch is also wonderful for shaping and adding extra body to hats.

Tailor's ham If you don't have one already, run out and buy a ham! A *tailor's ham* is a heavy, tightly stuffed pillow that is the size and shape of the well-known pork cut. Because human heads are round, most hat seams involve curves. The firm tailor's ham acts like a 3-D ironing board so you can neatly press as you sew.

Thread Use *all-purpose thread* in coordinating colors to make the stitching blend right into the hat, or use contrasting colors to make topstitching stand out.

TERMINOLOGY/TECHNIQUES

If you've ever made a quilt, garment, or handbag, you are likely familiar with many of the subjects discussed in this section. Some of the terms and techniques appear over and over again throughout the book, while others are only applicable to one or two projects.

Backstitching Stitching back and forth at the end of a seam to lock the threads in place.

Basting stitches Long, loose stitches that can be used for gathering or simply holding fabric in place for future stitching steps. Make sure the bobbin thread tension is set very low (1 or 2), but not all the way down to 0. Use the longest straight stitch length possible.

Curved piecing Curved piecing is required for many of the intermediate–advanced projects in this book. As opposed to working with straight edges, curved edges require a bit of manipulation. At first glance, it might look like two pieces aren't going to fit together. Use the notches and corners for initial placement, then align the edges in between. Gently stretch the edges, if needed. Use lots of pins and stitch slowly to avoid misalignment or puckering. After stitching, you might be instructed to snip or trim the seam allowance so that it lies properly. *Always press sharply curved seams on a tailor's ham.*

Edgestitching Topstitching that is sewn *very* close to an edge or seam. Use a regular presser foot to position the needle about ⅟₁₆" from the edge or seam. You can use special attachments like an edgestitching foot, ditch-quilting foot, or a blind hemming foot to control stitch placement.

Free-motion sewing For this technique, you are machine stitching, but you are in control of the direction of stitching. Use a darning or free motion foot. Lower or cover the feed dogs as described in your machine's owner's manual. Set the machine to make a medium-length straight stitch. Use your hands to guide the fabric as you stitch in the desired pattern.

Gathering Run two parallel rows of basting stitches. Pull the bobbin threads to make tiny, even gathers in the fabric. Do not pull on the needle threads at all, because that will cause the stitching to tighten up and ultimately break.

Double topstitching Double topstitching gives perfect parallel lines of topstitching to your hat. To achieve this, you will need both a *double* (also known as *twin*) *sewing needle* (either Universal 100 or Jeans) and an edgestitching presser foot for your sewing machine. Increase the stitch length to 3.5 for prominent stitching. If you don't have a second spool of topstitching thread, wind a bobbin with your existing topstitching thread. Place topstitching threads on separate spool holders. If you do not have separate spool holders, stack the bobbin of the topstitching thread on top of the larger spool.

Thread your sewing machine as you normally would with the first topstitching thread to the left needle, making sure the thread lies between the inner tension discs (if visible). Thread the second topstitching thread using the outside tension discs. Bypass the final thread guide just above the needle, then thread the right needle. **NOTE:** Your specific sewing machine instructions may differ slightly, so refer to your manual for proper twin needle threading, if needed.

Running stitch Running stitch is the most basic of hand stitches. Start by threading the needle and tying a knot in the end of the thread. Stick the needle into one side of the fabric and draw it through until the knot is at the insertion point. Reinsert to form a stitch. Repeat the process, alternating sides, to make the desired length of evenly spaced stitches. (See Figure 1 on the next page.)

Sealing ribbon ends Prevent the fraying of cut ends by treating them with a liquid seam sealant (described above), or by heat sealing. To **heat seal,** pass the end of the ribbon very quickly through a flame. For thicker ribbons, you may have to make several passes. For delicate ribbons like chiffon, simply holding the frayed end near the flame may be sufficient. You can also use a wood-burning tool for heat sealing.

Serger stitching A serger is a machine that nicely cuts and edge finishes fabric. This is not necessary for any of the projects in this book. However, if you own a serger, then you can use it as an alternative to zigzag stitching to finish straight seams.

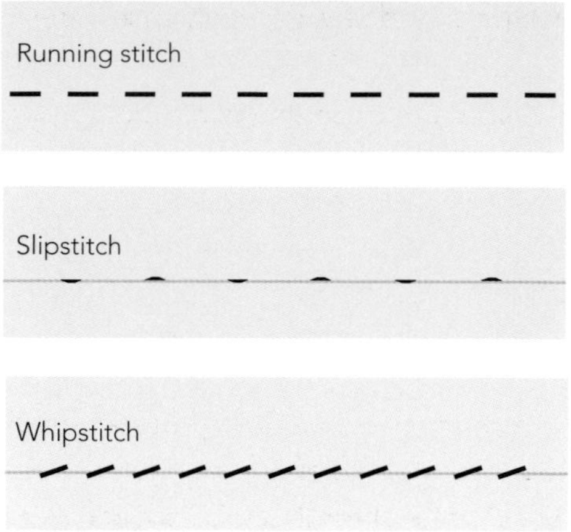

Running stitch

— — — — — — — — —

Slipstitch

Whipstitch

FIGURE 1

Slipstitching Slipstitching is used to invisibly close a seam. Thread a hand needle with a length of thread and tie a knot at the end. Insert it so that the knot ends up on the inside of the hat at the position of the seam. Work the needle back and forth between the layers, keeping the thread on the inside so that the stitches do not show. Tie a knot at the end of the stitching, and then bury the end in the seam. (See Figure 1.)

Starching a finished hat For best results, test spray a swatch of fabric to make sure it is suitable for starching. To add just a bit of body and crispness, lightly spray the hat and let dry, then press where needed. For heavier starching, you can fully saturate the hat with spray. Let dry, periodically hand shaping into the desired silhouette. A form like an upside-down bowl or bucket is great for drying hat crowns. Once the hat is dry, press and steam as needed, shaping as you go.

Topstitching This is a row of regular straight stitching that is sewn near a seam on the outside of a garment. Topstitching adds durability and detail to the seam.

Whipstitch Whipstitching is a quick and effective method to close a seam on the inside of a hat. Thread a hand needle with a length of thread and tie a knot at the end. Insert the needle so that the knot ends up on the inside of the hat. Work the needle back and forth between the layers, making angled stitches at the position of the seam. Tie a knot at the end of the stitching, and then bury the end in the seam. (See Figure 1.)

Working with knits For most knits, a universal needle works just fine. If you are working with something especially stretchy, you may need to use a stretch or ball-point needle. When straight stitching on knits, you should have a medium to long stitch length (I usually go with a setting between 3.5–4mm). If the stitch length is too small, the stitches will stretch out the fabric, resulting in puckering. Unless specifically told to do so, avoid stretching the fabric as you sew—just let it feed through the machine naturally. You can use narrow zigzag stitches in place of straight stitching for piecing, but keep in mind that the seams may have a "laddered" appearance if the seam is pulled open or topstitched.

Zigzag stitching Use medium-width zigzag stitching on a raw edge to finish and prevent fraying. You can substitute serger stitching for finishing with zigzag stitching.

Fabrics and Interfacings

FABRIC

The best part of making your own hats is choosing the fabric. Just wander around the fabric store and you will see that the options are truly endless. By varying fabric weight or texture, you can get completely different hats from a single pattern. For example, the Delmar Driving Cap is light and sporty when made from a crisp cotton, but rustic and substantial when made from a thick corduroy or wool. Suggested weights and specific fabric possibilities are provided within each hat's pattern, but don't be afraid to experiment. The hats in this book are made from three basic classes of fabrics: wovens, knits, and felts.

1. **Woven Fabrics** *Lightweight quilter's cottons* (also called *quilting cottons, quilt-weight cottons,* or *calicos*) are much beloved for their easy handling and the amazing array of designer and novelty prints. Paired with the right lining or interfacing (see below), you can use these fabrics to make just about any type of hat. Other readily available woven fabrics include batiks, broadcloths, ginghams, and homespuns. Fashion fabrics like wool and corduroy come in a wide range of weights and looks. Don't limit yourself to the garment sewing section either. Home decor fabrics make for wonderful hats.

2. **Knit fabrics** Knits are a natural choice for warm, cozy hats. The stretch of the fabric allows for a close fit and sizing flexibility. From soft interlocks to fuzzy fleeces, there are so many great knit solids and prints available. All of the knit fabric hats in this book are very easy to make. If you've never worked with knit fabric before, then hats are a great place to start. Tips for sewing/working with knit fabrics are provided earlier in this chapter.

3. **Felt** Because of its pliability, felt is very well suited for hat making. As with the other materials, it comes in different weights and fiber compositions. For the hats in this book, **wool felt** is recommended because it breathes and is a dream to work with.

INTERFACINGS

Choosing interfacing for a hat is a little different than choosing interfacing for a garment or handbag. For your typical coat or tote, the interfacing is selected based on the fabric type so that it will provide structure, and move and drape properly. In a hat, the interfacing works against gravity by bolstering up the fashion fabric to the needed degree. For most of the structured hats in this book, a thicker interfacing is fused to the brim and/or lining to provide a 3-D shape when the pieces are assembled. Because the brim is small and heavily stitched, and the lining is on the inside, fabric/interfacing compatibility is not so important. Rather, a specific weight of interfacing is selected to make the hat sturdy without adding unnecessary bulk or weight. In a few of the hats, the interfacing is fused to directly to the fashion fabric so that it will behave more like a thicker fabric. In these cases, the recommended interfacing will adhere without puckering, bubbling, or distorting the fabric. For every hat that requires an interfacing, a type/weight is suggested in the instructions, and descriptions and brand possibilities are listed underneath. Many wonderful stabilizers are on the market, and if you have a favorite that is not listed, by all means use it. *NOTE: Most interfacings are sold in 20–22" widths, and this is reflected in the yardage requirements. If your interfacing of choice happens to be 45" wide, you will need a little over half as much.* Always follow the manufacturer's recommendations for fusing (which should be on the packaging or yardage backing), and let pieces cool completely before proceeding to assembly.

- **Extra Firm Double-sided Fusible Interfacing:** very thick, stable (almost board-like) interfacing that is coated on both sides so it's perfect for stiff cap brims. Possibilities include: Dritz® InnerFuse™ and Pellon® Peltex® II.

- **Extra Firm Sew-in Interfacing:** more of an interlining than an interfacing, this material provides internal structure. Possibilities include: Pellon® Peltex® 70 and Pellon® Extra-Firm.

- **Fusible Fleece:** a batting-like material that gives a bit of puff and thickness to the fashion fabric without adding stiffness. Possibilities include: Pellon® Fusible Fleece, HTC Fusible Fleece, and Pellon® Thermolam®.

- **Fusible Webbing:** Used to adhere two layers of fabric together. Possibilities include: Pellon® Wonder-Under®, Steam-A-Seam® Fusible Web, and Dritz® Stitch Witchery.

- **Lightweight Fusible Interfacing:** thin, almost tissue-like, non-woven backing for light fabrics. Possibilities include: Thermoweb HeatnBond® Light Weight, Pellon® Fusible Featherweight, and Pellon® Fusible Sheerweight.

- **Medium- to Heavyweight Fusible Interfacing:** a broad category of thicker, paper-like interfacings that are great for providing structure to brims and linings. Possibilities include: Pellon® Decor Bond™, Pellon® Craft-Fuse™, and Pro-Woven Super Crisp™ Fusible Interfacing.

- **Tricot Knit Fusible Interfacing:** soft, very fluid interfacing that works well with most fashion fabrics. It adds an extra layer of thickness to the material and also gives a nice finished look to the back. Possibilities include: Fusi-Knit™ Fusible Tricot Interfacing, Pellon® Easy-Knit Fusible Tricot Interfacing, and Pro-Tricot Deluxe™ Interfacing.

- **Woven Cotton Fusible Interfacing:** a light cotton fabric that can be fused to quilt-weight fabrics, adding thickness without distortion. Possibilities include: Pro-Woven Shirt-Crisp™, Bosal Fashion Fuse™, and Pellon® Shape-Flex®.

Sizing

This book contains patterns for tiny babies all the way up to adult women and men. For each hat, a specific size range is given at the beginning of the pattern. The hat sizes in this book are standardized for consistency across patterns. The table in Figure 2 provides a general sizing guide for the hats in this book. Basically, a comfortable-fitting hat needs to be about an inch bigger than the head circumference. For knit or elasticized hats, however, the actual hat size should be *smaller* than the head circumference in order to ensure a snug fit. Use a measuring tape to measure the circumference of the hat recipient's head, just above the ears, as shown in Figure 3. Then choose the size in Figure 2 that is closest to the head circumference measurement. For best results, make a test hat from an inexpensive fabric, just like you would make a muslin for garment fitting.

Size	Head Circumference	Sizing Category					
		Baby	Toddler	Child	Youth	Woman	Man
NB	Less than 18"	SMALL					
XXS	18½"–19½"	LARGE	SMALL	SMALL			
XS	19¾"–20½"		LARGE	AVERAGE	SMALL		
S	20¾"–21½"			LARGE	AVERAGE	SMALL	
M	21¾"–22¼"				LARGE	AVERAGE	SMALL
L	22½"–23"					LARGE	AVERAGE
XL	23¼"–23¾"					X-LARGE	LARGE

Age Ranges:
Baby: 0–6 months
Toddler: 6–36 months
Child: 3–6 years
Youth: 7–14 years
Adult: 15+ years
FIGURE 2: Hat Sizing Table

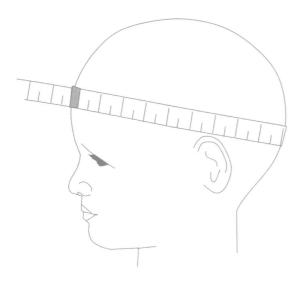

FIGURE 3: Measuring Head Circumference

CHILDREN'S SIZES

Kids' head sizes are as unique and unpredictable as kids themselves, so it is important to measure a child's head when making a hat for him or her. When my son was a baby, his body was a bit smaller than average, yet his head was in the ninety-ninth percentile. Now that he is 6, his body is starting to catch up, but his noggin still measures on the large side. On the other hand, our neighbor is a tall, 10-year-old girl, and her head is a full inch smaller than my son's head. They both look (and usually act) like normal kids, but their hat sizes are different than one would predict from a simple size chart. Keep in mind that young kids' heads grow very quickly. The average baby's head expands almost 4" in the first year! If you are making a hat for a child who is between sizes, go with the larger of the two. To make hats for newborns and small infants, you can easily scale the patterns down on a photocopier. To convert the XXS to a NB (18" circumference), scale down to 95%. To convert the XXS to an XXXXS (17" circumference), scale down to 90%. Keep in mind that some hat styles are not suited to babies who are not yet sitting up, and babies will outgrow little hats very quickly.

ADULT SIZES

The average female's head circumference falls in the medium range, and the average male's head circumference falls in the large range. In general, taller people have larger heads, but this isn't always the case. My husband and I are both of short stature, and my head measures in the small range, while his measures in the extra-large range (now is a good time to mention that there is only a slight correlation between cranial capacity and intellect 😊). Hair is also a factor when determining which hat size to make. A full, curly head of hair takes up more room than a bald head. Again, it is important to measure to get the right fit. In this book, most of the hats designed for women go up to size L, and the hats designed for men (but are still suitable for women) go up to size XL. If the recipient of the hat has a head that measures larger than the pattern sizes, you can scale the patterns up on a photocopier. To convert a L to an XL, enlarge 104%. To go up to an XXL (24½" head circumference), scale the XL up 105%. To go up to an XXXL (25½" head circumference), scale the XL up 109%.

Guide to Illustrations and Patterns

ILLUSTRATIONS

Each hat project's first figure illustrates the cutting layout, which is provided not only for placement purposes, but also to give a visual representation of the number and type of pieces needed to make the hat. (See Figure 4.) If a pattern piece is placed on or near a dashed line labeled "fold," then it means that the fabric must be folded at this position before cutting. If the pattern is placed *on the fold line,* you will get a symmetrical piece that is twice the size of the original pattern. If the pattern is placed *near the fold line,* you will get two mirror-image pieces.

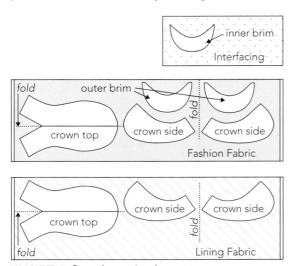

FIGURE 4: Sample cutting layout

For most projects, the main fashion fabric is a solid color. If the fabric has a "wrong" side, it is shaded the opposite of the main fashion fabric (white with small dots of the same solid color). Lining fabrics are represented by a diagonal stripe—the wrong side has a lighter-colored stripe than the right side. (See Figure 5.) For reversible hats, the stripe represents the second fashion fabric. Contrasting fabrics are usually grey, but other colors are used if needed to represent multiple fabrics. Interfacings are white with grey dots. The cutting layouts are a good reference for determining which color/texture corresponds to a particular fabric in the hat.

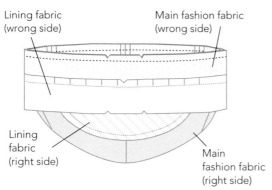

Lining fabric
(wrong side)

Main fashion fabric
(wrong side)

Lining
fabric
(right side)

Main
fashion fabric
(right side)

FIGURE 5: Color scheme explanation

Dashed lines represent straight stitching. For basting stitches, the dashes are longer and farther apart than regular stitches. The stitches are darker and thicker in the illustrations that show their *initial* placement. In *subsequent* illustrations, these stitches will still be visible, but will be lighter and thinner. (See Figure 6.)

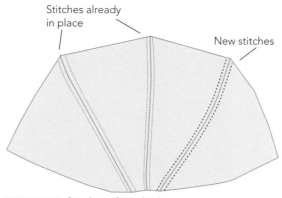

Stitches already
in place

New stitches

FIGURE 6: Stitching line thickness

In some cases, a single illustration shows two parts of a step (usually pinning and stitching)—the first on the left-hand side, and the second on the right-hand side. *However, **each part** of the illustration step should be performed on **both** sides of the hat.* (See Figure 7.)

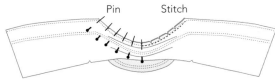

FIGURE 7: Two steps within one figure

Some illustrations might also show a series of images to represent each task that you will perform within one step, as shown in Figure 8.

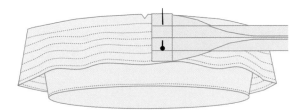

Pin tape into place

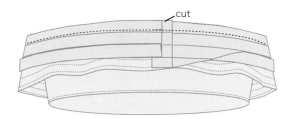

Align, stitch, and cut

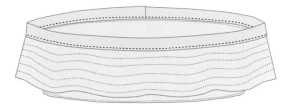

Fold and stitch

FIGURE 8: Multiple steps within one figure

PATTERNS

Pattern pieces for each pattern (except for those hats that are cut to specific dimensions) are located online at www.wiley.com/go/sewnhats. The pattern sets are contained within separate PDF files. Open the file for the desired project and print all of the pages onto letter-sized paper. **NOTE:** The patterns are designed so that you can print them at 100%. Before printing the patterns, make sure your printer's page scaling is set to "none" in the Adobe Acrobat print window. In order to make sure that your patterns will print at the correct size, measure the box on the first pattern page. It should measure exactly 1" × 1". After printing, overlap the sheets at the indicated points, and tape, glue, or staple together.

Each pattern piece is labeled with the hat title, and specifies the number of pieces to cut and the type of fabric to use. (This information is also included under the "Cut the Pattern Pieces" heading within each pattern.) For multi-sized patterns, a different patterned line represents each size. The corresponding sizes are clearly marked beside the lines. The edges that should be placed on folds are labeled as well. Make sure you also cut any notches or transfer any markings that are indicated on the pattern pieces.

STAYING COOL

Sunny Days Hat

SUNNY DAYS HAT

By Patty Young (MODKID Designs)

Pool parties, bike rides, and playgrounds fill every little girl's summer social calendar. Bring on the summer festivities with this fun, flirty, and super-sweet reversible sunhat sized to fit baby girls and schoolgirls alike. Have fun mixing and matching fabric patterns and adding whimsical ribbon trims . . . the possibilities are endless!

Sizes: XXS–S (Baby–Child)

Skill Level: Beginner/Intermediate

Materials

- 1 fat quarter (18" × 22") or ¼ yard each of 4 different fashion fabrics for the hat wedges. The designer used cotton prints from Patty Young's Grand Bazaar collection. Other possibilities include canvas, lightweight denims or corduroys, mediumweight decorator fabrics, muslins, or quilter's cottons. (For more info on fabric types, see chapter 1.)
- ⅛ yard light- to mediumweight fabric for the ruffled brim
- ½ yard lightweight fusible interfacing (see chapter 1) to back the wedges on one side of the hat). NOTE: If you would like to interface the wedges on both sides of the hat, you will need 1 yard.
- 1 yard of ¾"–⅞"-wide grosgrain or jacquard ribbon. Patty Young's line of reversible jacquard ribbons are perfect for this project!
- Washable marker for marking buttonholes
- OPTIONAL: Two ½"-wide shank-style decorative buttons or a button kit with ½"-wide fabric-covered buttons

Cut the Pattern Pieces

From *each* wedge fabric: Cut 3 pieces using the wedge pattern. You should have 12 total wedges.

From the ruffle fabric: Cut a 4" × 43" strip.

From the lightweight fusible interfacing: Cut 6 pieces using the wedge pattern.

From the ribbon: Cut a 20½" length for size XXS, a 22" length for size XS, or a 24" length for size S.

Assemble the Hat

1 Following the manufacturer's instructions, apply fusible interfacing to the wrong side of 6 of the wedge pieces that you will piece together on one side of the hat. Choose the side with the lightest colors because the interfacing will help prevent the underside of the fabric from showing through on the right side of the hat. Use the washable marker to mark the position of the buttonholes on the right side of the fabric as indicated on the wedge pattern. **NOTE:** If desired, you can interface all the wedges, but keep in mind that this will create a stiffer hat.

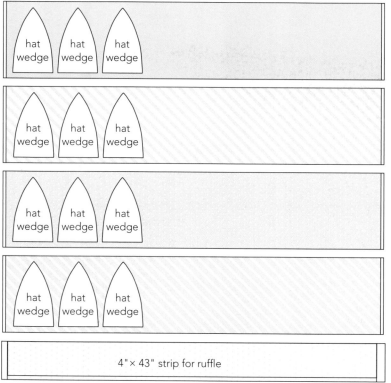

FIGURE 1: Cutting Layout

2 Choose the 2 fabrics you want on the outside side of the hat and lay them out in alternating fashion. Place 2 alternating pieces together, right sides facing, and pin together. Stitch ½" in from one of the curved side edges. (See Figure 2.)

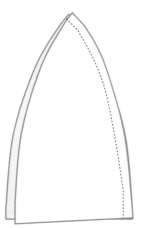

FIGURE 2

3 Use your iron to press the seam allowance open. To this pair, align one side of the next alternating piece, right sides facing, and pin. Stitch ½" from the aligned edges. (See Figure 3.)

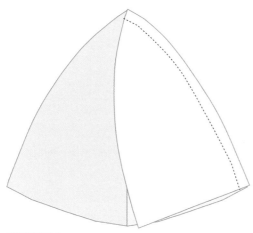

FIGURE 3

4 Press the seam allowance open. You should now have 3 alternating fabrics stitched together. Set this hat half aside. Pin and stitch the remaining 3 pieces in the same manner.

5 Place the 2 halves of your hat right sides together and align the outer edges, making sure to match the center seams. Pin the layers together, then stitch along the curved edge with a ½" seam allowance. (See Figure 4.) Press the seam allowance open to complete your first hat dome.

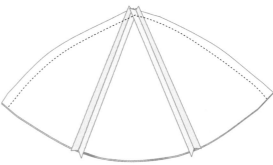

FIGURE 4

6 Repeat steps 2–5 with your other set of alternating fabrics to make the dome for the reverse side of the hat.

7 Fold the brim strip in half widthwise, right side facing in. Stitch together, ½" from the aligned short edges. Press the seam allowance open.

8 Fold the joined strip in half lengthwise, wrong side facing in, and press. (See Figure 5.)

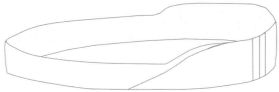

FIGURE 5

9 Run a row of basting stitches ¼" from the raw edges. *Do not backstitch because you will need the threads loose for gathering the fabric to form a ruffle.* (See Figure 6.)

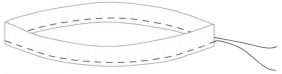

FIGURE 6

10 Carefully pull the loose-hanging basting thread to gather your brim into a ruffle that is the same circumference as the base of your finished hat domes. Use your fingers to evenly distribute the fabric.

11 Slip the ruffle (either side since the hat is reversible) over the right side of one of your hat domes (either one). Align the raw edges and pin. Stitch the ruffle into place, ¼" from the aligned edges. (See Figure 7.)

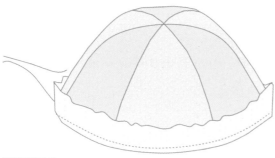

FIGURE 7

12 With the right sides together, place the second dome over the first dome, making sure that the ruffled brim is sandwiched between the layers. Pin, then stitch ½" from the bottom of the hat, leaving a 4" gap unstitched. (See Figure 8.)

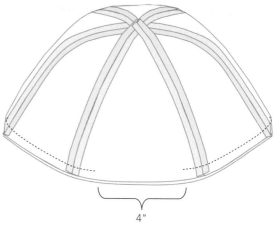

4"

FIGURE 8

13 Turn the hat right side out through the opening and tug on the brim all around to make sure the edges are fully turned out. Arrange the opening so that it is folded flush with the rest of the bottom edge and press. Slipstitch the opening closed using a hand needle and matching thread. Press around the perimeter of the hat, then topstitch along the dome ⅛" from the seam.

14 Pin the layers of the hat together at the position of the seams to prevent shifting. Using the proper foot and following the manufacturer's instructions for your particular sewing machine, make the 12 buttonholes at the marked positions. Using your seam ripper or small sharp scissors, carefully cut a 1" slit where indicated in each buttonhole. (See Figure 9.)

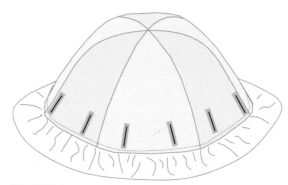

FIGURE 9

15 Weave the ribbon in and out of each buttonhole until the ends meet on one side. (See Figure 10.)

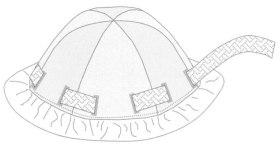

FIGURE 10

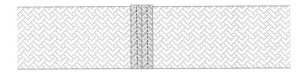

FIGURE 11

16 Stitch the two ends, same sides together, with a ¼" seam allowance. Tuck the raw edges of the ribbon under and then topstitch them in place. (See Figure 11.) **NOTE:** The MODKID woven label is stitched right over that seam (on both sides of the hat) to further secure the ribbon in place and cover the seam. You can use your own label or simply tack the ribbon into place, if desired.

17 **OPTIONAL:** For added whimsy, you can embellish the hat with a couple of ½"-wide decorative or fabric-covered buttons. On each side of the hat, sew a button into place at the very tip where all six wedges meet.

French General
Sunhat

FRENCH GENERAL SUNHAT

By Kaari Meng (French General)

Whether you are walking through the lavender fields of Provence or relaxing by the sea in St. Tropez, this hat will protect your skin and make you look très chic. The wide brim features a kettle edge that you can flip up or down depending on the sun or the occasion. An optional drawstring in the inner band allows for the perfect fit. This hat has great structure and a crisp look when worn, but is flexible enough to fold up for travel.

Sizes: Adjustable to sizes S–L (Youth–Adult)

Skill Level: Beginner/Intermediate

Materials

- **Main fashion fabric:** 1 yard lightweight to mediumweight woven fabric. The designer used vintage striped ticking in this project, but you can use solids or prints as well. Other possibilities include canvas, linen, quilter's cottons, or twill.
- **Lining fabric:** ½ yard lightweight woven fabric
- 1½ yards heavyweight fusible interfacing (see chapter 1)
- OPTIONAL: 2 yards of 1½"-wide grosgrain ribbon, plus liquid seam sealant (such as Fray-Check®) or a cigarette lighter for sealing ends
- OPTIONAL: 1 yard cotton cording for inside drawstring
- OPTIONAL: Basting tape

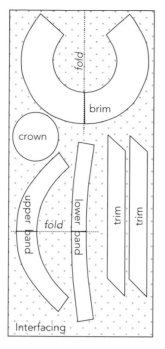

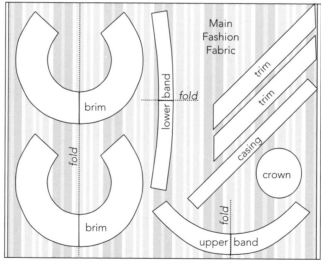

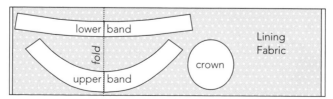

FIGURE 1: Cutting Layout

Cut the Pattern Pieces

From the main fashion fabric: Cut 1 piece from the crown pattern. Cut 2 pieces from the brim pattern (on folds). Cut 1 piece each from the upper band and lower band patterns (on folds). Cut 2 pieces from the trim pattern and 1 piece from the casing pattern on the bias (a 45-degree angle relative to the selvage).

From the lining fabric: Cut 1 piece from the crown pattern. Cut 1 piece each from the upper band and lower band patterns (on folds).

From the heavyweight fusible interfacing: Cut 1 piece from the crown pattern. Cut 1 piece each from the brim, the upper band, and the lower band patterns (on folds). Cut 2 pieces from the trim pattern (parallel to the long edge of the interfacing).

Assemble the Hat

1 Fuse the heavyweight interfacing to the wrong sides of 1 brim piece, 2 trim pieces, the lining upper band, and the lining lower band according to the manufacturer's instructions.

2 **For the fashion fabric (non-interfaced) band pieces:** Place the upper and lower band pieces together, right sides facing. Align the single center notches and pin together at this position. Match the ends and the other notches, and align and pin the edges in between. **NOTE:** If needed, you can gently stretch the edges of the lower band to meet the curved edges of the upper band. Stitch together, ¼" from the aligned edges. (See Figure 2.)

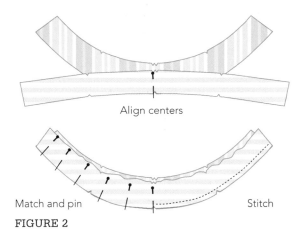

Align centers

Match and pin   Stitch

FIGURE 2

3 With an iron, press the seam allowance up against the upper band. Topstitch along the upper band, ⅛" from the seam. Fold the outer band assembly in half widthwise, right side facing in. Stitch ¼" from the aligned short edges. (See Figure 3.) Press the seam allowance open.

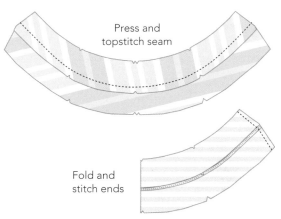

Press and topstitch seam

Fold and stitch ends

FIGURE 3

4 **For the fashion fabric crown and outer band assembly:** With the right sides facing, match the notches and seam of the curved upper band with the notches of the crown and pin. Align and pin the edges in between. Stitch the crown to the band, ¼" from the aligned edges. Press the seam allowance against the upper band. Topstitch along the upper band, ⅛" from the seam. (See Figure 4.)

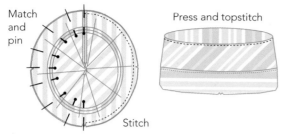

Match and pin

Press and topstitch

Stitch

FIGURE 4

6 Join the lining (interfaced) upper and lower band pieces as described in step 2, but omit the topstitching. Attach the lining crown to the lining band assembly as described in step 4, but again, omit the topstitching.

7 Fold the short ends of the casing piece over ¼" to the wrong side and press. Stitch into place, ⅛" from the folds. Fold in half lengthwise, wrong side facing in, as shown in Figure 6.

5 Fold the outer (non-interfaced) brim piece in half widthwise, right side facing in. Stitch ¼" from the aligned short edges. Slip the brim over the outer hat top so that the right sides are facing and the inner raw edges are in line with those of the lower band. Match the seams and notches and pin into place. Align and pin the edges in between. Stitch ¼" from the aligned edges. Flip the brim down and press the seam allowance up against the band. Topstitch along the band, ⅛" from the seam. (See Figure 5.)

Fold and stitch ends

Fold in half lengthwise

FIGURE 6

8 Turn the lining hat top so the right side is facing out. Align the double notches in the casing with those of the lower hat band and pin into place. Stretch the casing over to match the single notches and pin. Butt the ends together at the back seam and pin into place. Align and pin the edges in between the notches and seams. Stitch the casing into place, ⅛" from the aligned edges. (See Figure 7.)

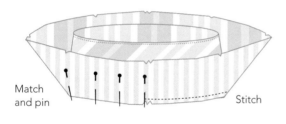

Match and pin

Stitch

Press and topstitch

FIGURE 5

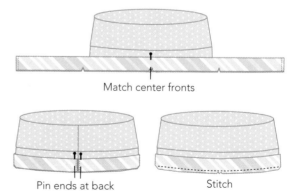

Match center fronts

Pin ends at back

Stitch

FIGURE 7

9 Fold the inner brim piece in half widthwise, right side facing in. Stitch ¼" from the aligned short edges. Slip the brim over the inner hat top so that the right sides are facing and the inner raw edges are in line with those of the lower band and casing. Match the seams and notches and pin into place. Align and pin the edges in between. Stitch ¼" from the aligned edges. Flip the brim down and press the casing and seam allowance up against the band. (See Figure 8.)

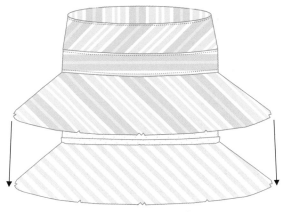

Slip outer hat over inner hat

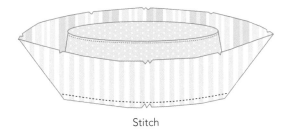

Stitch

Stitch

FIGURE 9

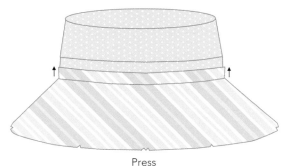

Press

FIGURE 8

10 Place the outer hat top over the inner hat top with the wrong sides facing. Match the seams and notches, and align the edges. Stitch the layers together, ⅛" from the aligned edges. (See Figure 9.)

11 Place the trim strips together with the right sides facing and notches in line. **NOTE:** The notches don't have to line up perfectly; they just need to be on the same side. Rotate the top strip 90 degrees so that the short edges are in line on one side. Arrange the short ends so there are ¼" overhangs on each side. Stitch together, ¼" from the aligned edges. This will give you a single strip with all the notches on the same side. Press the seam allowance open and trim away the overhangs. (See Figure 10.)

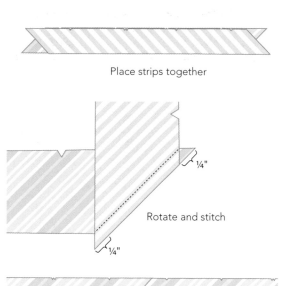

Place strips together

Rotate and stitch

¼"

¼"

Press

FIGURE 10

12 Fold the strip in half lengthwise, wrong side facing in, and press to make a crease. Unfold, then fold the un-notched edge over ¼" to the wrong side and press. Unfold that edge and join the ends as described in the previous step in order to make a loop. (See Figure 11.)

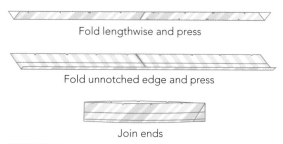

Fold lengthwise and press

Fold unnotched edge and press

Join ends

FIGURE 11

13 With the right sides facing, match the notches in the trim with those of the outer hat. Align the edges in between and pin together. Stitch ¼" from the aligned edges. (See Figure 12.)

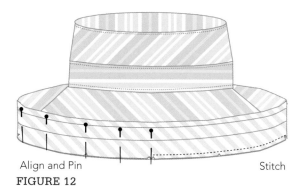

Align and Pin   Stitch

FIGURE 12

14 Refold the trim at both creases. Flip the hat over to the inner side, and finger press the seam allowance down against the trim. Align the folded edge with the stitching from the previous step. Baste into place with hand stitching or basting tape. Working on the outer side of the hat, topstitch the trim into place, ⅛" from the seam. (See Figure 13.)

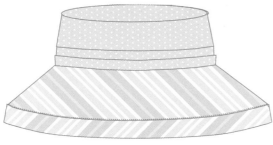

Align and Baste

Topstitch

FIGURE 13

15 Tie the cording into a knot at one end. Wrap the other end with tape to prevent fraying. Use a safety pin to insert the taped end of the cording into the casing. Remove the tape and tie a knot.

16 **OPTIONAL:** Heat seal or apply liquid sealant to the ends of the ribbon (see chapter 1 for instructions). Wrap the ribbon around the band of the hat, and tie a bow in the back.

Basic Bucket
Hat

BASIC BUCKET HAT

By Carla Crim (Scientific Seamstress)

You will have buckets of fun wearing this utilitarian, yet stylish hat. It's the perfect hat for activities like fly-fishing, camping, boating, or just strolling along the dock. So, if you want to make a go-to hat for the outdoorsy types in your life, consider using a simple, durable fabric like khaki or canvas. If you prefer to get your exercise in a retail setting, consider using fun prints and embellishments to make a fashion statement. You can even add eyelets for extra ventilation and design detail. This classic hat style is suitable for all ages and personalities!

Sizes: XXS–XL (Baby–Adult)

Skill Level: Beginner/Intermediate

Materials

- ⅜ yard medium- to heavyweight woven fashion fabric (60" width is typical). The designer used denim and home decor fabric for this project. Other possibilities include canvas, corduroy, or duck cloth.

    OR

- ½ yard lightweight fabric (like quilter's cotton or broadcloth, typically 45" wide) **and** 1 yard tricot knit fusible interfacing (see chapter 1).
- 1 package ½"-wide single fold bias tape in a color that coordinates with the fabric
- 1 package ½"-wide double fold bias tape in a color that coordinates with the fabric
- Glue stick (see chapter 1)
- Basting tape (see chapter 1) or needle and thread for hand basting
- OPTIONAL: Four ⁵⁄₃₂" eyelets and eyelet-making tool

Cut the Pattern Pieces

From the fabric: Cut 1 piece from the crown pattern. Cut 2 pieces from the band pattern. Cut 4 pieces from the brim pattern.

From the interfacing (*if using a lightweight fabric*): Cut 1 piece from the crown pattern. Cut 2 pieces from the band pattern. Cut 4 pieces from the brim pattern.

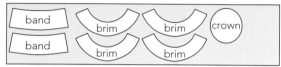

FIGURE 1: Cutting Layout

Assemble the Hat

1 If working with a lightweight fabric, fuse the interfacing to the wrong side of all pieces following the manufacturer's instructions.

2 **OPTIONAL EYELETS:** Transfer the dots on the band pattern to the wrong sides of the band pieces. Apply eyelets according to the manufacturer's instructions.

3 Place the 2 band pieces together, right sides facing, and align the edges. Stitch together, ¼" from each of the short side edges. Trim the raw edges slightly and press open. (See Figure 2.) Cover the seams with single fold bias tape as described in the sidebar (below).

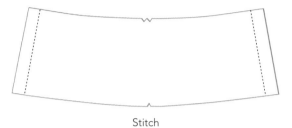

Stitch

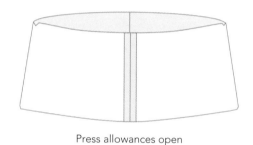

Press allowances open

FIGURE 2

Covering a Seam with Single Fold Bias Tape

Working on the wrong side, apply glue (using a glue stick) to the trimmed and pressed seam allowance. Cut a piece of single fold bias tape that is a bit longer than the seam. Place the bias tape over the seam, making sure the centers are perfectly in line. Press to set. If you are working with a curved seam, make sure you use a tailor's ham (see chapter 1). Working on the right side of the fabric, stitch ⅛" from both sides of the seam. Check the wrong side to make sure the stitching properly caught the tape at the folds. Trim the tape so it is flush with the top and bottom edges of the fabric.

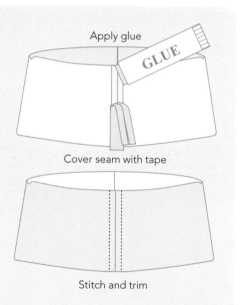

Apply glue

GLUE

Cover seam with tape

Stitch and trim

4 With the right sides facing, match the double notches in the band with those of the crown. Match the band seams with the single notches in the crown. Align and pin the edges in between. Stitch the crown to the band, ¼" from the aligned edges. (See Figure 3.)

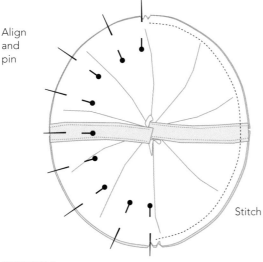

Align and pin

Stitch

FIGURE 3

5 The next step is to finish the seam with double fold bias tape. You can either cut a piece of tape that is a few inches longer than the crown's perimeter, or just work from the roll of tape. Cut the tape so the end is nice and straight, then unfold a few inches. Fold the end over ½" to the wrong (inner) side and press with your iron. Place the right side of the tape against the wrong side of the band, and align the raw edges. Pin into place near one of the double notches. Start stitching the tape into place ¼" from the edges, aligning the tape with the band and crown edges as you go. When you reach the original fold, stitch over it by ¼", then backstitch. Cut the bias tape at the end of the stitching, ¼" beyond the original fold. (See Figure 4.)

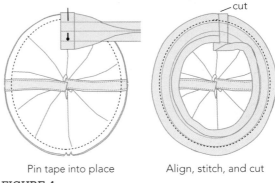

cut

Pin tape into place   Align, stitch, and cut

FIGURE 4

6 Refold the tape over the seam allowance. The folded end should neatly overlap the raw end. Working on the crown side, arrange the folded edge of the tape so it is in line with the stitching. Stitch through all layers, ⅛" from the folded edge. Turn the hat top right side out, and press the encased seam allowance down against the band. Topstitch to set into place, ⅛" from the seam. (See Figure 5.)

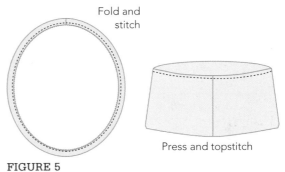

Fold and stitch

Press and topstitch

FIGURE 5

7 Place 2 of the brim pieces together, right sides facing, and align all of the edges. Stitch ¼" from each of the short side edges. Press the seam allowances open. Repeat with the other pair of brim pieces. Place the 2 brim assemblies together, right sides facing, and align the edges, matching the notches and the seams. Align the edges and pin. Stitch together, ¼" from the outer edges. Trim the seam allowance down to ⅛". Turn the brim right side out. Work the outer edge between your fingers to fully roll out the seam and press. Topstitch ⅛" from the outer edge. Run a second line of topstitching ¼" from the first. Repeat the topstitching process until you are about ½" from the inner edge of the brim. (See Figure 6.)

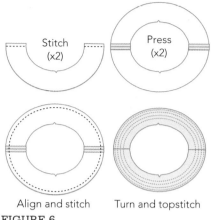

Stitch (x2)

Press (x2)

Align and stitch

Turn and topstitch

FIGURE 6

Finishing a Hat with Double Fold Bias Tape

The right (outside) side of the brim should be flipped up against the right side of the hat. Cut a piece of double fold bias tape that is a few inches longer than the perimeter of the opening edge, or just work from the carded tape. Cut the tape so the end is straight, then unfold a few inches. Fold the end over ½" to the wrong (inner) side and press. Place the right side of the tape against the wrong side of the brim, and align the raw edges. Pin into place near the center back notch. Start stitching the tape into place ¼" from the edges, aligning the tape with the brim and band edges as you go. When you reach the original fold, stitch over it by ¼", then backstitch. Cut the tape at the end of the stitching. Refold the tape over the seam allowance. The folded end should neatly overlap the raw end. Working on the inner side of the hat, arrange the folded edge of the tape so it is in line with the stitching. For best results, secure with basting tape or hand baste into place. Stitch through all layers, ⅛" from the folded edge.

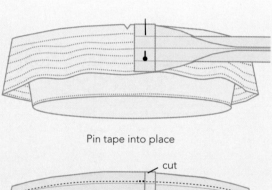

Pin tape into place

cut

Align, stitch, and cut

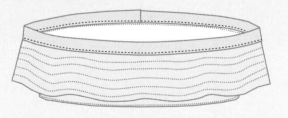

Fold and stitch

8 Slip the brim over the band so that the right side (the one that will be on top in the finished hat) of the brim is facing the right side of the band. Match the seams and the notches, and align the edges in between. Pin the layers together. Stitch together, ¼" from the aligned edges. (See Figure 7.) Cover the seam allowance with double fold bias tape as described in the sidebar on the previous page.

9 Turn the hat top right side out, and press the encased seam allowance up against the band. Topstitch to set into place, ⅛" from the seam. (See Figure 8.)

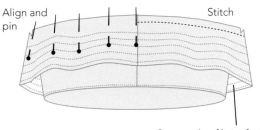

Align and pin

Stitch

Outer side of brim facing outer side of band

FIGURE 7

Topstitch

FIGURE 8

Summer
Blossom
Sunhat

SUMMER BLOSSOM SUNHAT

By Joanna Figueroa (Fig Tree & Co.)

This lightweight sunhat is perfect for frolicking in the garden on a hot summer's day. The scalloped brim frames her face like a ring of pretty petals while providing shade from the sun's rays. This hat can be made from a mixed bouquet of fabrics, or stick with a single variety for a solid look. Add a covered button to top off the crown. A sweet set of ties is a practical and adorable option.

Sizes: XXS–S (Baby–Youth)

Skill Level: Beginner/Intermediate

Materials

- **Fabric:** Light- to mediumweight woven fabric in coordinating prints and/or solids. The designer used Fig Tree quilter's cottons for this project. Other possibilities include broadcloth, homespuns, linen, or quilter's cottons.
  - ¼ yard for the outer hat wedges
  - ¼ yard for the outer brim
  - ½ yard for the lining (inner hat wedges and brim underside)
  - OPTIONAL: ⅛ yard for the ties
- ½ yard lightweight fusible interfacing (see chapter 1)
- 1 package of ½"-wide double fold bias tape in a coordinating color
- Washable pencil or marker for outlining scallop shapes
- OPTIONAL: ½"- to ¾"-wide fabric-covered button kit

Cut the Pattern Pieces

From the outer wedge fabric: Cut 6 pieces using the wedge pattern.

From the outer brim fabric: Cut 2 pieces using the brim pattern (on folds).

From the lining fabric: Cut 6 pieces using the wedge pattern. Cut 2 pieces using the brim pattern (on folds).

From the lightweight fusible interfacing: Cut 2 pieces using the brim interfacing pattern (on folds).

From the tie fabric (optional): Cut a 1¼" × 40" length.

Assemble the Hat

1 Place 2 outer fabric wedges together, right sides facing, and pin along one long edge. Stitch together along this edge, ¼" from the aligned edges. Press the seam allowances open. Place another outer wedge atop the existing pair, right sides facing, and align and pin one long edge. Stitch and press as described for the first pair. Set this assembly aside, and repeat the steps with the remaining 3 outer wedges. Put the 2 assemblies together, right sides facing, and align both curved sides. Pin together, making sure the seams match. Stitch together, ¼" from the curved side edges. (See Figure 2.)

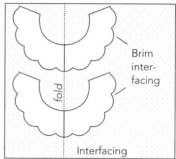

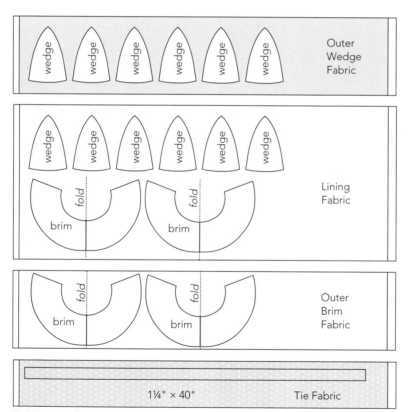

FIGURE 1: Cutting Layout

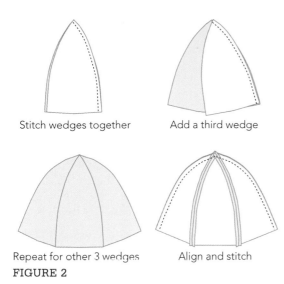

Stitch wedges together   Add a third wedge

Repeat for other 3 wedges   Align and stitch

FIGURE 2

2 Repeat step 1 with the lining fabric wedges.

3 Place the completed crowns together, wrong sides facing. Match the seams and align the bottom edges. Pin, then stitch together, ⅛" from the aligned edges. (See Figure 3.)

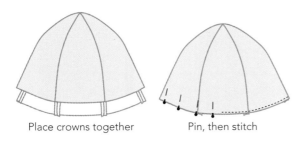

Place crowns together   Pin, then stitch

FIGURE 3

4 **For each lining brim piece:** Place a scalloped interfacing piece on the wrong side and align the inner curved edges. Fuse according to the manufacturer's instructions. Let cool, then make sure the scalloped edges are well adhered to the fabric. **OPTIONAL:** Use your washable pencil or marker to lightly trace around the interfacing's scallops on the wrong side of the fabric in order to

make the edges more visible during the stitching process. Place the 2 lining brim pieces together, right sides facing. Stitch together, ¼" from the aligned short edges. (See Figure 4.) Trim the seam allowance down to ⅛".

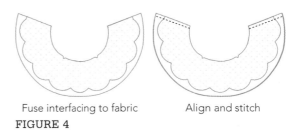

Fuse interfacing to fabric   Align and stitch

FIGURE 4

5 Place the 2 **outer** brim pieces together, right sides facing. Stitch together, ¼" from the aligned short edges. Trim the seam allowance down to ⅛".

6 Place the inner and outer brim assemblies together, right sides facing. Match the seams and align the outer edges. To reduce bulk, arrange the seam allowances so they are pointing in opposite directions on different sides. Baste stitch together, ⅛" from the outer edges. Using tight, tiny stitches, stitch just **outside** the scalloped edge of the interfacing. Start in the "valley" of a scallop and pivot at the peaks. (See Figure 5.)

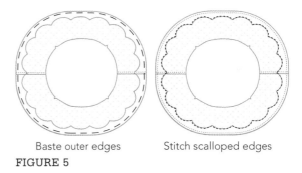

Baste outer edges   Stitch scalloped edges

FIGURE 5

7 Use your scissors to make snips from the outer raw edge of the brim to the dips between the scallops, taking care to not clip the stitching. Trim the seam allowances around the scallops down to ⅛".

Turn the brim right side out. Work the scalloped edge between your fingers to fully roll out the seams. Gently tug on the scallops to minimize any puckering at the dips. Press, then topstitch ⅛" from the outer scalloped edges. (See Figure 6.)

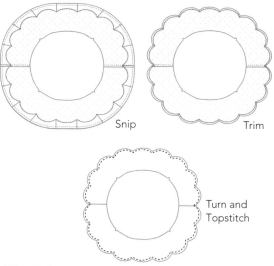

Snip   Trim

Turn and Topstitch

FIGURE 6

8 With the outer side of the brim facing the outer side of the crown, align the raw edges. Match the seams and notches in the brim with the seams in the crown. Pin together. Stitch together, ¼" from the aligned edges. (See Figure 7.) To add ties, proceed to the next step. Otherwise, finish the edge with double fold bias tape as described on page 38.

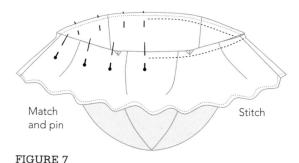

Match and pin   Stitch

FIGURE 7

9 OPTIONAL: Lay out the strip of fabric for the tie with the wrong side facing up. Fold in half lengthwise, wrong side facing in, and press to make a crease. Unfold. Bring both raw edges over to meet the crease, wrong side facing in again. Press. Bring the folded edges together so that the raw edges are on the inside. Stitch ⅛" from the folded edges. (See Figure 8.)

Fold strip lengthwise and press, then unfold

Fold long edges to meet crease

Fold lengthwise and stitch

FIGURE 8

10 Cut the stitched strip in half to make 2 ties of equal length. Tie 1 end of each of the pieces in a knot, and trim at an angle. Stitch the tie to the brim lining side of the exposed seam allowance, right at the position of the brim seam. (See Figure 9.) Finish the edge with double fold bias tape as described in the sidebar on page 38.

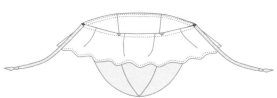

FIGURE 9

Oasis Flap Cap

OASIS FLAP CAP

By Carla Crim (Scientific Seamstress)

Whether you are trekking the dunes or building a sandcastle, this cool cap will keep the sun's warm rays at bay. The long brim and back flap protect sensitive skin much better than any sunscreen will, and the lightweight fabric breathes even on the hottest days. This is a great opportunity to use those fun novelty batiks or preppy embroidered seersuckers (think turtles, frogs, and palm trees). You can even upcycle Grandpa's favorite outgrown madras-plaid beach shirt into something that will protect his bald head (you'll have to find something else to cover his belly).

Sizes: XXS–XL (Baby–Adult)

Skill Level: Beginner/Intermediate

Materials

- ½ yard lightweight woven fabric (that does not have an obvious wrong side). The designer used batiks for this project. Other possibilities include solid quilter's cottons, madras, seersucker, or nylon ripstop. For additional UV protection, prewash the fabric with a UV protectant laundry treatment, such as Rit SunGuard™.
- ¼ yard heavyweight fusible interfacing (see chapter 1)
- ½"-wide single fold bias tape
- ½"-wide double fold bias tape
- ¼"-wide elastic
- Safety pin to insert elastic
- Glue stick (for single fold bias tape finishing)

Cut the Pattern Pieces

From the fabric: Cut 1 piece from the center cap pattern (on a fold). Cut 2 pieces each from the side cap pattern and the brim pattern. Cut 1 flap piece to the appropriate dimensions given in Table 1.

From the heavyweight fusible interfacing: Cut 2 pieces from the brim pattern.

Elastic: Cut 1 piece of elastic to the appropriate length shown in Table 1.

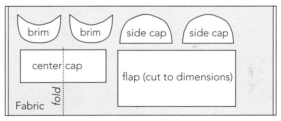

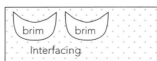

FIGURE 1: Cutting Layout

TABLE 1: FLAP DIMENSIONS AND ELASTIC LENGTHS

Size	Flap Piece Dimensions	Elastic Length
XXS	16"W × 7"H	2¼"
XS	17¾"W × 7½"H	2½"
S	18¼"W × 7¾"H	2¾"
M	19"W × 8"H	3"
L	19½"W × 8¼"H	3¼"
XL	20"W × 8½"H	3½"

Assemble the Hat

1 Following the manufacturer's instructions, fuse the interfacing to the wrong sides of both brim pieces.

2 With the right sides facing, match the middle notch in one of the side cap pieces with the middle notch in the center cap piece. Pin together. Match and pin the other two notches and the ends. Align the edges in between and pin. Stitch ¼" from the aligned edges. Repeat with the other side piece. Trim the seam allowance slightly, then press open. Finish the seams with single fold bias tape as described in the sidebar on page 36. (See Figure 2.)

3 Place the brim fabric pieces together, right sides facing. Stitch together along the un-notched side, ¼" from the edge. Use your scissors to snip about 4 notches near each curve along the seam allowance. Turn right side out and work the edges between your fingers to fully roll out the seam. Press. Topstitch ¼" from the seam. (See Figure 3.)

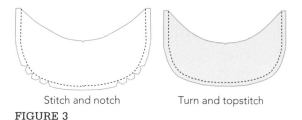

Stitch and notch　　　Turn and topstitch

FIGURE 3

4 With the right side of the cap's top front facing the right side of the brim (the side that will be on top in the finished hat) align the notches and pin together. Align the adjacent edges of the brim with those of the crown. Use lots of pins to prevent gaps or wrinkles from forming. Zigzag stitch to set the brim into place. Remove the pins. Straight stitch ¼" from the zigzag stitched edges. (See Figure 4.)

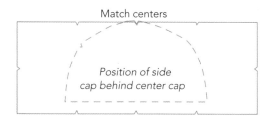

Match centers

Position of side cap behind center cap

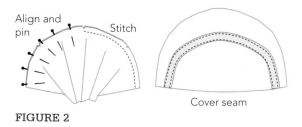

Align and pin　　Stitch

Cover seam

FIGURE 2

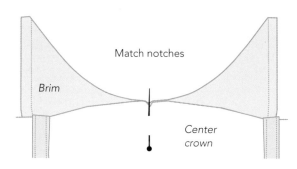

Match notches

Brim

Center crown

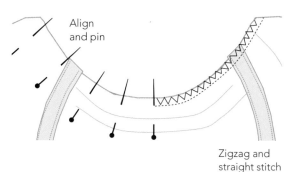

Align and pin

Zigzag and straight stitch

FIGURE 4

5 For each of the short sides of the flap, fold the edge over ¼" to the wrong side and press. Fold the bottom long edge of the flap over ¼" to the wrong side and press. Repeat the folding process on the sides, then the bottom again. Stitch the folds into place, ⅛" from the edges. (See Figure 5.)

FIGURE 5

6 Turn the cap right side out. With the right side of the flap facing the right side of the crown, align the raw edges of the flap with those of the cap. Bring the ends of the flap over to meet the ends of the brim and pin. Align and pin the edges in between. Stitch ¼" from the aligned edges. Finish the seam with double fold bias tape as described in the sidebar on page 38. Flip the band up and topstitch along the crown, ⅛" from the seam. (See Figure 6.)

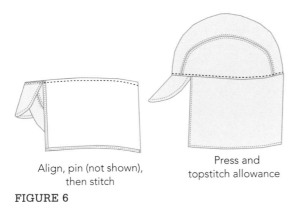

Align, pin (not shown), then stitch

Press and topstitch allowance

FIGURE 6

7 Edgestitch the top edge of the double fold bias tape against the crown between the two back seams (which are covered with single fold bias tape). Start the stitching at one cap seam, and end it on the outer edge of the other cap seam, making sure to backstitch at the beginning and end. Use a safety pin to insert the elastic into the casing formed by the edgestiching. Draw the elastic through until the end of the elastic is about ½" from the first seam. Stitch into place by sewing back and forth at the position of the seam. Pull the elastic through to the other seam and remove the safety pin. Adjust the elastic so that the end of the elastic is about ½" beyond the second seam. Stitch into place at the position of the seam. (See Figure 7.)

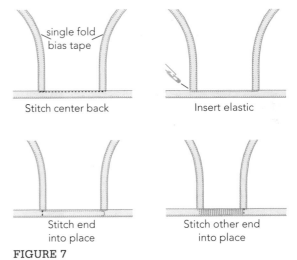

single fold bias tape

Stitch center back

Insert elastic

Stitch end into place

Stitch other end into place

FIGURE 7

Cut the Pattern Pieces

From the outer fabric: Cut 1 piece each from the front and back band patterns (on folds). Cut 1 brim piece on the bias (oriented at a 45-degree angle relative to the selvage edge).

From the inner fabric: Cut 1 piece each from the front and back band patterns (on folds). Cut 1 brim piece on the bias (oriented at a 45-degree angle relative to the selvage edge).

From the fusible interfacing: Cut 2 pieces from the front band pattern (on folds). Cut 2 pieces from the brim interfacing pattern.

From the extra firm interfacing: Cut 1 piece from the brim interfacing pattern.

From the elastic: Cut to the appropriate length: Size XS = 5", Size S = 6", Size M = 7", Size L = 8".

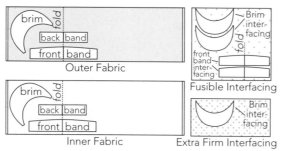

FIGURE 1: Cutting Layout

Assemble the Hat

1 Center the fusible brim interfacing pieces on the wrong sides of the inner and outer brim pieces. There should be a ½" distance between the edges all the way around. Fuse according to the manufacturer's recommendations. Apply the fusible band interfacing to the inner and outer front band pieces in the same manner.

2 Place the 2 brim pieces together, right sides facing, and align all of the edges. Pin, then stitch together, ½" from the *front* curved edges.

Trim the seam allowances down to ¼" and snip near the curves, taking care not to cut the stitching. (See Figure 2.)

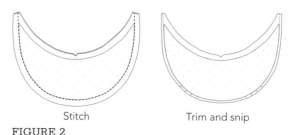

Stitch   Trim and snip

FIGURE 2

3 Turn the brim right side out. Work the edge between your fingers to fully roll out the seam. Press. Insert the extra firm interfacing piece between the inner and outer band pieces. Work the brim around the facing snugly. The top edge of the interfacing should be in line with the already fused interfacing inside the brim. If needed, trim the top edge down slightly. Using a long, loose basting stitch, sew ½" from the *inner* edge of the brim. Snip the resulting seam allowance with cuts every ½" or so. Topstitch ¼" from the *outer* edge of the brim. (See Figure 3.)

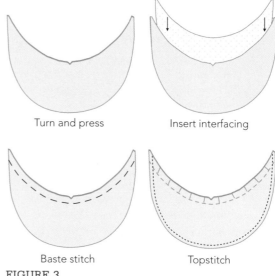

Turn and press   Insert interfacing

Baste stitch   Topstitch

FIGURE 3

4 Fold the un-notched long edge of the *outer* front band over ½" to the wrong side. Repeat with the *inner* front band. (See Figure 4.)

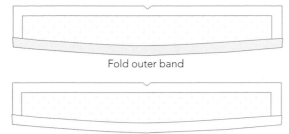

Fold outer band

Fold inner band

FIGURE 4

5 Place the right side of the outer fabric **front band** on the outer fabric side of the **brim.** Match the notch in the outer front band with the notch in the assembled brim. Using lots of pins, align and pin the adjacent edges. With the brim side against the feed dogs, baste stitch ½" from the aligned edges. *Stitch slowly, taking care to avoid puckering. It is helpful to let the brim curl a bit inwards into the shape that you will see in the finished visor.* Pin the outer band to the brim in the center. (See Figure 5.)

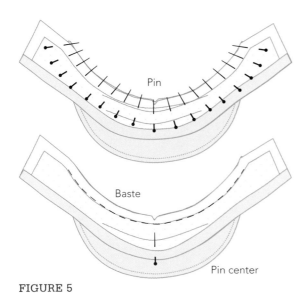

Pin

Baste

Pin center

FIGURE 5

6a With the right sides facing, place the *inner* front band piece on the *outer* front band piece, sandwiching the brim in between. Match and pin at the position of the notches. Align and pin the adjacent edges, using lots of pins, all the way to the ends. With the front band against the feed dogs, stitch (this time with a normal stitch length) ½" from the aligned edges. Again, take care to avoid puckering on each side. Snip the resulting allowance to match that of the brim. Use a seam ripper to remove any visible basting stitches on the exterior of the visor. (See Figure 6a.)

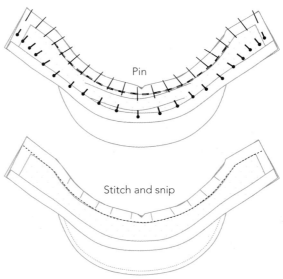

Pin

Stitch and snip

FIGURE 6a

6b Press the seam allowance open at the ends of the front band/brim assembly. (See Figure 6b.)

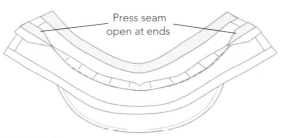

Press seam open at ends

FIGURE 6b

7 Place the back band pieces together, right sides facing. Stitch together, ½" from the long edges on one side. Press the seam allowance open. Fold the unsewn long edges over ½" to the wrong side. Press. (See Figure 7.)

Stitch, then press

Fold and press

FIGURE 7

8 Unfold the ½" folds near the ends of both the front and back band assemblies. Align one end of the back band with one end of the front band. The right sides should be facing, and the inner and outer fabrics should match up. Stitch together, ½" from the aligned edges. Repeat on the other side. Press the seam allowances open, then refold the ½" folds. (See Figure 8.)

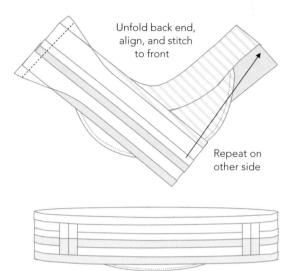

Unfold back end, align, and stitch to front

Repeat on other side

Press and refold

FIGURE 8

9 Bring the inner and outer bands together, wrong sides facing. Align and pin the folded edges all the way around. If needed, rearrange the fold in the inner band to match that of the outer band. Stitch together, ¼" from the aligned edges. Topstitch ¼" from the bottom edge of the band as well. (See Figure 9.)

Pin

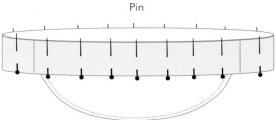

Topstitch

FIGURE 9

Insert elastic

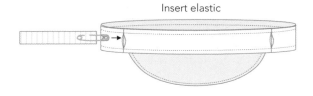

Stitch, pull, pin

Tuck in end and stitch

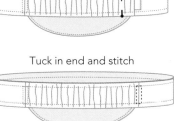

FIGURE 10

10 Use a seam ripper to pick out the band seam stitching on the inner side, between the rows of topstitching. Use a safety pin to insert elastic into the back band through the openings. Position one end of the elastic ½" beyond the seam in the direction of the brim. Secure by stitching in a box shape, ⅛" from either side of the seam between the two rows of topstitching. Pull the elastic through the opposite opening and remove the safety pin. Arrange the end of the elastic so it is ½" beyond the opening and pin. Tuck the end into the band and then stitch into place as described for the previous side. (See Figure 10.) Slipstitch the openings closed.

KEEPING WARM

Fleece Beanie

Extreme Altitude Cap

Turn It Up Hat

Stocking Cap

Quick Snuggle Hooded Scarf

Oooh-la-la Beret

Fleece Beanie

FLEECE BEANIE

By Jennifer Hagedorn (Tie Dye Diva Designs)

In the time it takes to drink a grande mocha latte, you can knock out this cuddly warm beanie. You can make the pieced crown from a single solid or printed fleece fabric, or you can have fun alternating colors. You can use matching or contrasting fleece for the band as well. Teeny beanies are wonderful for little ones. You can top one off with a cute pom-pom or add a big fleece flower to make a perfect photo prop. For bigger folks, you can make a sleek and stylish beanie. It's a good thing this beanie is so quick and easy to sew, because everybody is going to want one!

Sizes: XXS–L (Baby–Adult)

Skill Level: Beginner

Materials

- **Main fabric:** ¼ yard polyester fleece for the crown (can use 2 different colors for alternating pieces, which requires ¼ yard each). The designer used blizzard fleece (generic Polar Fleece) for this hat.
- **Contrasting fabric:** ¼ yard polyester fleece for the band (will have enough left over for optional pom-pom)
- OPTIONAL: Fleece flower or fleece pom-pom embellishment (see the appendix for fabric requirements)

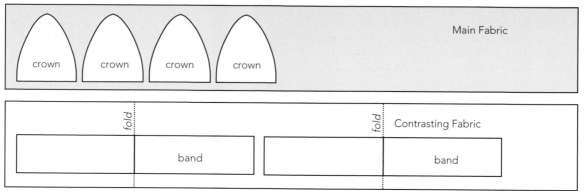

FIGURE 1: Cutting Layout

Cut the Pattern Pieces

From the main fabric: Cut 4 pieces from the crown pattern (all from same fabric for solid hat, or 2 from each of 2 fabrics for alternating option).

From the contrasting fabric: Cut 2 pieces from the band pattern (on a fold). **OPTIONAL:** Cut a 12" × 3" strip of fleece for a pom-pom, and/or cut flower circles (using the Fleece Flower Embellishment pattern pieces) for a fleece flower as described in the appendix.

Assemble the Hat

1 Place 2 crown pieces together, right sides facing. Stitch together, ¼" from the right-hand side edge. (See Figure 2.) Repeat with the other 2 crown pieces. *NOTE: If you are alternating colors, make sure to stack the colors in the same order for both pairs.*

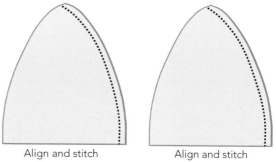

Align and stitch   Align and stitch

FIGURE 2

2 Place the 2 crown halves together, right sides facing. Align the curved edges and pin the layers together. Stitch ¼" from the aligned edges. (See Figure 3.)

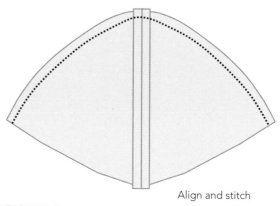

Align and stitch

FIGURE 3

3 Place the band pieces together, right sides facing. Stitch ¼" from each of the short edges. Fold the band in half lengthwise, wrong side facing in. Align the raw edges. You should have a skinny loop with the right sides facing out. (See Figure 4.)

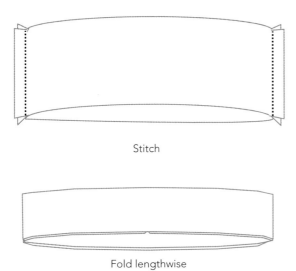

Stitch

Fold lengthwise

FIGURE 4

4 Slip the loop over the crown, with the right side (the one that will be on the outside of the finished hat) of the band facing the right side of the crown. Align and pin the raw edges, matching the side seams of the band to those of the crown. Stitch ¼" from the aligned edges. (See Figure 5.) Flip the band down and finger press the seam allowance up against the cap.

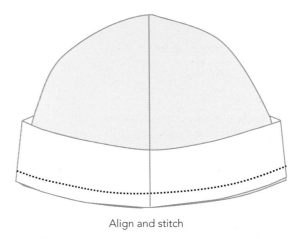

Align and stitch

FIGURE 5

5 **EMBELLISHMENT OPTION 1:** Create a fleece pom-pom as described in the appendix. Sew into place securely at the intersection of the seams on the top of the hat.

EMBELLISHMENT OPTION 2: Use the leftover fleece to make a fleece flower, as described in the appendix. Sew into place on the band.

EXTREME ALTITUDE CAP

By Carla Crim (Scientific Seamstress)

Up in a plane or atop a mountain (or even walking across a college campus in the frigid air) . . . this cap is designed to weather the harshest of climates. With a warm outer shell and soft fur lining, this classic trapper-style cap is a winter essential. You can wear it two ways: with the flaps down and covering the ears, or fastened at the top with ties. Optional pockets provide a place to store secret codes, spare change, or cough drops. This cap is a great way to use those plush corduroys and fun faux furs you've been eyeing (and admit it . . . snuggling) at the fabric store.

Sizes: XXS–XL (Baby–Adult)

NOTE: If you are using a very thick fur (1" pile, or more), use the next size up. If you are using a thinner fur (¼" pile, or less), go with the next size down.

Skill Level: Intermediate

Materials

- ½ yard medium- to heavyweight woven fashion fabric. The designer used corduroy for this project. Other possibilities include velvet, denim, or canvas.
- ½ yard faux fur. **NOTE:** You can use a stretchy fur (like furry fleece or minky), but purchase and fuse a heavyweight interfacing (see chapter 1) to the back before cutting.
- OPTIONAL: glue stick (for pocket addition)
- OPTIONAL: ½ yard ribbon or cording (⅛" to ½" wide) for tie

Cut the Pattern Pieces

From the woven fabric: Cut 2 mirror-image pieces from the center cap pattern (near a fold). Cut 1 piece from the brim pattern. Cut 2 pairs of mirror-image pieces (4 total) from the cap side pattern (near a fold). Cut 2 flap pieces (near a fold). Cut 2 pocket pieces (near a fold, optional). *NOTE: You should cut the flap and pocket pieces on the bias, so make the fold at a 45-degree angle relative to the selvage edge. If you are working with a napped fabric, make sure to orient the nap downward as shown in Figure 1.*

From the fur: Cut pieces as described for the woven fabric, but orient the flaps *with* the grain rather than the bias, and omit the pockets.

From the ribbon or cording: Cut two 9"-long pieces.

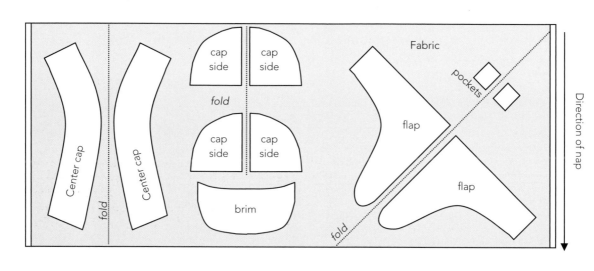

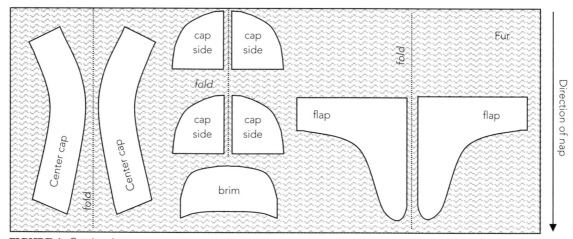

FIGURE 1: Cutting Layout

Assemble the Hat

1 **For each pocket (optional):** Fold the top short edge of the pocket piece over ½" to the wrong side and press. Stitch ⅜" from the fold. Fold the long side edges over ¼" to the wrong side and press. Make and glue a ¼" fold in the bottom edge. *TIP: Use a bit of glue from a glue stick to set the folds.* Position the wrong side of the pocket on the right side of the fabric flap piece as indicated on the pattern piece. Pin into place. Topstitch around the side and bottom, ⅛" from the folded edges. Make sure you backstitch at the beginning and end of the stitching. (See Figure 2.)

2 **For each tie (optional):** Use a liquid seam sealant, such as Fray Check™, or heat seal both ends of the tie (see chapter 1). Lay the tie on the right side of the fabric flap piece with the end of the tie about ½" below the bottom tip of the flap. Stitch into place, ⅛" from the edge of the fabric. (**OPTIONAL:** Make a knot near the end of the tie.) Fold up the tie, and pin it to the fabric to keep it out of the way during the stitching process. (See Figure 3.)

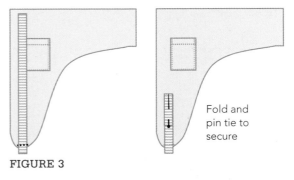

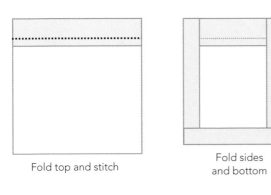

Fold top and stitch

Fold sides and bottom

Fold and pin tie to secure

FIGURE 3

3 Place a pair of fabric cap side pieces together, right sides facing, and align all of the edges. Stitch together, ¼" from the notched edges. Press the seam allowance open, and topstitch ⅛" from both sides of the seam. (See Figure 4.) *Repeat for the other pair of cap side pieces.*

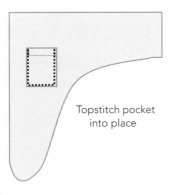

Topstitch pocket into place

FIGURE 2

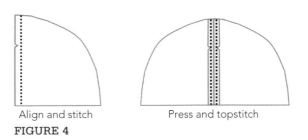

Align and stitch

Press and topstitch

FIGURE 4

4 With the right sides facing, match the seam in the top (curved) edge of 1 **cap side assembly** with the notch in a **center cap** piece. Match the ends, and align and pin the edges in between. Stitch together, ¼" from the aligned edges. (See Figure 5.) *Repeat with the other cap side assembly and center cap piece.*

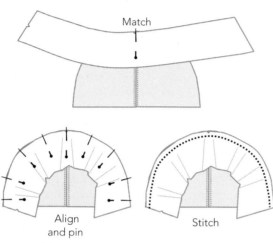

Match

Align and pin

Stitch

FIGURE 5

5 **For both center/cap side assemblies:** Press the seam allowance open, and topstitch ⅛" from **both** sides of the seam. Place the fabric center/cap side assemblies together, right sides facing, and align the long curved center edges. Stitch together, ¼" from the aligned edges. Press the seam allowance open, and topstitch ⅛" from **both** sides of the seam. (See Figure 6.)

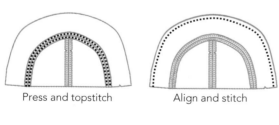

Press and topstitch

Align and stitch

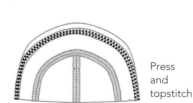

Press and topstitch

FIGURE 6

6 Repeat the cap top assembly process with the fur pieces, but finger press the seam allowances open, and eliminate the topstitching steps.

7 Place the **brim** (fabric and fur) pieces together, right sides facing, and align all of the edges. Pin together, using lots of pins. Stitch ¼" from the un-notched outer edges. Snip the seam allowance near the curves. Turn the brim right side out. Work the edges between your fingers to fully roll out the seam. If needed, use a pin to pick the fur out of the seam. Press the brim piece. (See Figure 7.)

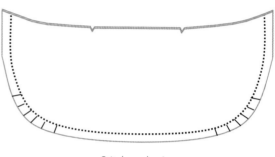

Stitch and snip

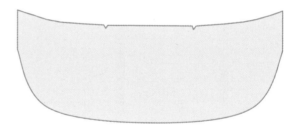

Turn and press

FIGURE 7

8 Place the brim on the fabric crown assembly. The right fabric sides should be facing and the notches should be matched. Align the edges and pin into place. Use a zigzag stitch to set the edges together. (See Figure 8.)

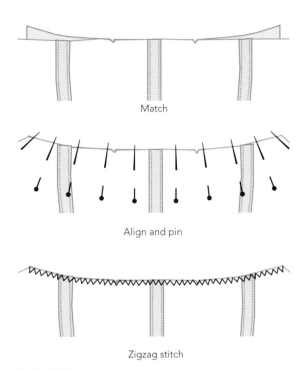

Match

Align and pin

Zigzag stitch

FIGURE 8

9 Place the **woven fabric flap** pieces together, right sides facing, and align all of the edges. Stitch together, ¼" from the short back edges. Press open the seam allowance, and topstitch ⅛" from *both* sides of the seam. (See Figure 9.) *Repeat the assembly process with the* **fur flap** *pieces, but finger press the seam open, and eliminate the topstitching step.*

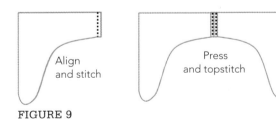

Align and stitch

Press and topstitch

FIGURE 9

10 Place the earflap assemblies together, right sides facing, and align all of the edges. Pin together, using lots of pins. Stitch together, ¼" from the curved side and bottom edges. Snip the seam allowance near the curves (except at the position of the ribbon/cord tie, if applicable). Turn the piece right side out. Work the edges between your fingers to fully roll out the seam. If needed, use a pin to pick the fur out of the seams. Align the top raw edges. Stitch the layers together, ⅛" from the aligned edges. (See Figure 10.)

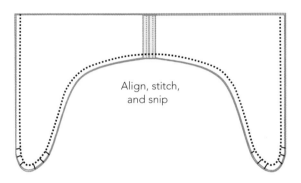

Align, stitch, and snip

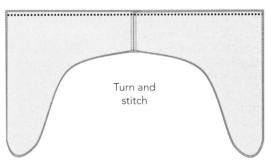

Turn and stitch

FIGURE 10

11 Turn the cap right side out with the brim turned up against the cap. Place the earflap on the fabric cap assembly. Make sure the fabric sides are facing and the back seams are in line. The ends of the earflap assembly should touch the ends of the brim. Align the edges and pin into place. Use a zigzag stitch to set the edges together. With right sides facing, slip the fur cap assembly over the fabric cap assembly. Match the notches and seams, and align the edges. The cap

assemblies should fit together like nested bowls. Pin the layers together, making sure the earflap ends are tucked inside so that they will not get caught in the stitching. Stitch ¼" from the aligned edges, leaving a 2" opening in the center back. (See Figure 11.)

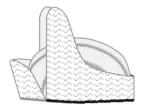

Zigzag stitch earflap to crown

Put crowns together

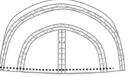

Align and stitch

FIGURE 11

12 Turn the hat right side out. Whipstitch (see chapter 1) the opening closed. Topstitch along the crown, ⅛" from the seam. **OPTIONAL:** Tack the brim into place against the crown. (See Figure 12.)

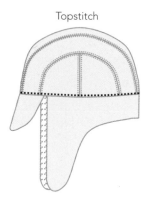
Topstitch

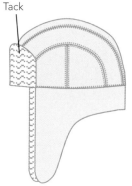
Tack

FIGURE 12

Turn It Up Hat

TURN IT UP HAT

By Shelly Figueroa (Figgy's Patterns)

This close-fitting, stylish hat is easy to make and oh-so-comfortable. You can flip the single-piece brim up all the way to the top of the crown, or pull it down a bit lower to get a different look. Depending on your choice of stretchy knit fabric, this hat can be sleek and lightweight, or thick and toasty warm. An optional gathered fabric rosette (see the appendix for pattern/construction info) adds sweetness and interest to the brim.

Sizes: S–L (Youth–Adult)

NOTE: If you are working with a thick fabric, you may wish to make a larger size than usual.

Skill Level: Beginner

Materials

- ¾ yard stretch knit fabric for the hat. The designer used interlock for this hat. Other possibilities include fleece, jersey, or stretch velvet.
- OPTIONAL FABRIC ROSETTE EMBELLISHMENT: ⅛ yard light- to mediumweight woven fabric
- Universal ball-point needle for sewing knit fabric

Cut the Pattern Pieces

From the knit fabric: Cut 1 piece (on a fold) using the brim pattern. Cut 2 pieces using the crown pattern.

OPTIONAL: From the woven flower fabric, cut a 3" × 32" strip.

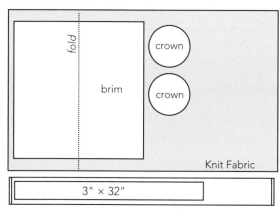

FIGURE 1: Cutting Layout

Assemble the Hat

1 With the wrong side facing in, bring the un-notched brim edges together. Stitch ½" from the aligned edges. With the right side facing in, fold the tube and align the notched edges. Pin the layers together. Run a basting stitch ¼" from the aligned edges. (See Figure 2.)

Align and stitch

Fold, align, and baste

FIGURE 2

2 Place the 2 crown pieces together, right sides facing. **NOTE:** If you are working with a knit that tends to curl, you may wish to baste stitch the crown pieces together, ¼" from the edge to stabilize.

3 Lightly gather the top of the brim. With the right (outer) sides facing, match the notches in the crown layers with the notches and seam of the brim layers and pin the layers together. *NOTE: If you are working with a directional print, keep in mind the majority of the brim will be flipped up, and the inner side will be showing.* Stitch the crown to the brim, ½" from the aligned edges. (See Figure 3.) Trim the seam allowance to ¼".

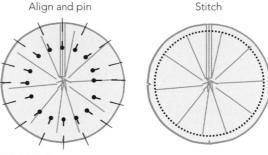
Align and pin   Stitch

FIGURE 3

4 Turn the hat right side out and flip up the brim.

5 **OPTIONAL:** Using the woven fabric strip, fold, gather, and sew a gathered fabric rosette to the brim as described in the appendix.

STOCKING CAP

By Jennifer Hagedorn (Tie Dye Diva Designs)

Here is a hat that is great for dashing through the snow or settling in for a long winter's nap. This fleece stocking cap is soft, cozy, and so easy to make. Classic red with white accents makes *the* perfect hat for Santa. And don't forget about the little elves! Go with green and red, or use non-traditional colors to make a fashion statement. Beyond the holidays, these hats are just the ticket for loyal sports fans. Use team colors or licensed prints to warm heads and hearts alike.

Sizes: XXS–L (Baby–Adult)

Skill Level: Beginner

Materials

- **Main fabric:** ½ yard polyester fleece for crown. The designer used blizzard fleece (generic Polar Fleece).
- **Contrasting fabric:** ¼ yard polyester fleece for band and pom-pom

Cut the Pattern Pieces

From the main fabric: Cut 1 piece from the crown pattern (on a fold).

From the contrasting fabric: Cut 1 piece from the band pattern (on a fold). Cut a 12" × 3" strip of fleece for the pom-pom.

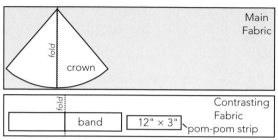

FIGURE 1: Cutting Layout

Assemble the Hat

1 Fold the crown piece at the center front with the right side facing in, and align the long raw edges. Pin, then stitch ½" from the aligned edges. (See Figure 2.) Trim the seam allowance down to ¼". Turn right side out. **NOTE:** See chapter 1 for *more information about sewing knit fabrics.*

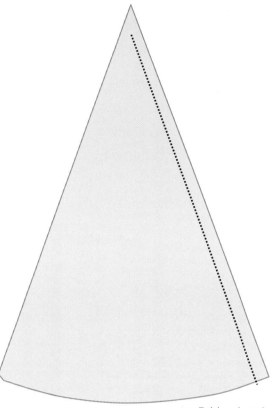

Fold and stitch

FIGURE 2

2 Fold the band piece in half widthwise, right side facing in. Stitch ½" from the short edges. Trim the seam allowance down to ¼". Finger press the seam allowance open. Fold the band in half lengthwise, wrong side facing in. Align the raw edges. You should have a skinny loop with the right sides facing out. (See Figure 3.)

Align and stitch

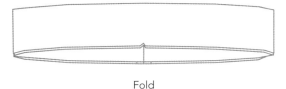

Fold

FIGURE 3

3 Slip the loop over the cap, with the right side (the one that will be on the outside of the finished hat) of the band facing the right side of the cap. Align and pin the raw edges, matching the notches and the seams. Stitch ½" from the aligned edges. (See Figure 4.) Trim the seam allowance down to ¼". Flip the band down and finger press the seam allowance up against the cap.

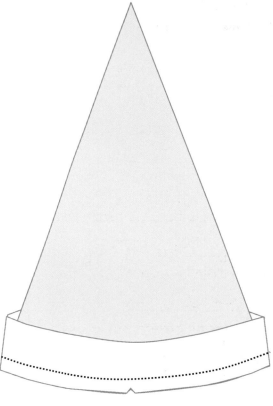

Align and stitch

FIGURE 4

4 Create the fleece pom-pom as described in the appendix. Sew into place securely at the tip of the hat.

Quick Snuggle
Hooded Scarf

QUICK SNUGGLE HOODED SCARF

By Carla Crim (Scientific Seamstress)

Who doesn't have time for a quick snuggle? This simple hood/scarf combo is easy to make and goes on and off in a snap. It is perfect for bundling up wiggly little ones on a cold day. And it's a great accessory for coats that don't have hoods, or you can layer it under a hooded jacket. The hood is reversible to give two different looks and feels against the skin. Pair a lighter knit with a thicker fleece for a mediumweight hood. For a heavier wrap, use two thick fabrics. You can add a pom-pom or tassel trim to the scarf ends for extra fun and cuteness.

Sizes: XXS–L (Baby–Adult)

Skill Level: Beginner

Materials

- ½ yard each of 2 different knit fabrics. The designer used fleece and interlock. Other possibilities include furry fleece, jersey, minky, or stretch velvet.
- OPTIONAL: ½ yard pom-pom or tassel trim

Cut the Pattern Pieces

From each knit fabric: Cut 2 mirror-image pieces from the side pattern (near a fold). Cut 1 piece from the center pattern (on a fold).

From the optional trim: Cut 2 pieces that are slightly smaller than the short ends of the side pieces. Make sure the pom-poms or tassels are centered on the piece. Trim away pom-poms/tassels at the ends so they will not be in the way of stitching.

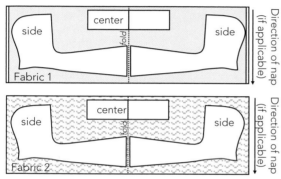

FIGURE 1: Cutting Layout

Assemble the Hat

1 **OPTIONAL:** If you are adding trim to the scarf ends, baste stitch it into place on the right sides of 1 set of side pieces (either set is fine). You should orient the trim so that the pom-poms/tassels are pointed towards the hood. Arrange the trim so that edge with the pom-poms/tassels is about ¼" from the short end of the scarf. (See Figure 2.)

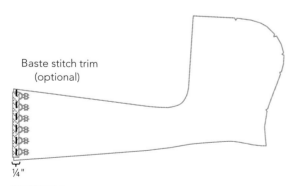

Baste stitch trim (optional)

¼"

FIGURE 2

2 Lay one of the **fabric 1 side** pieces out with the right side facing up. Place the **fabric 1 center** piece atop the side piece, right side facing down, and align the bottom corners. Working up towards the top, match and pin the notches. When you reach the end, match and pin the corners. Align and pin the edges in between. Stitch ¼" from the aligned edges. Add the second side piece (of fabric 1) to the center as described for the first, making sure the top and bottom are oriented correctly. Press the seam allowances open. *NOTE: If you are using a synthetic fabric like fleece, make sure you use a low iron setting to avoid scorching.* (See Figure 3.)

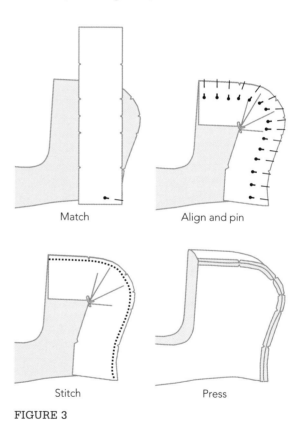

Match   Align and pin

Stitch   Press

FIGURE 3

3 Repeat step 2 with the fabric 2 pieces. Leave this assembly with the wrong side facing out, and turn the fabric 1 assembly right side facing out. Slip the fabric 2 assembly over the fabric 1 assembly, right sides facing. Align and pin the raw edges. Use lots of pins to prevent shifting during the stitching process. (See Figure 4.)

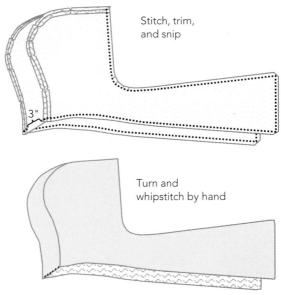

Stitch, trim, and snip

3"

Turn and whipstitch by hand

FIGURE 5

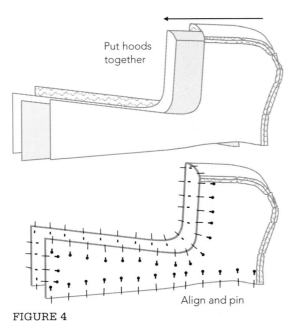

Put hoods together

Align and pin

FIGURE 4

4 Stitch ¼" from the aligned edges, leaving a 3" opening in the bottom of the center back. Snip the seam allowance at the curves, and trim the seam allowance at the corners. Turn the hooded scarf right side out through the opening. Work the seams between your fingers to fully roll out the seams. If needed, use the tip of a straight pin to pick out the corners. Press the edges using the proper iron temperature. Fold the edges under at the back opening so they are flush with the sides. Hand whipstitch the opening closed. (See Figure 5.)

Oooh-la-la Beret

OOOH-LA-LA BERET

By Carla Crim (Scientific Seamstress)

Bonjour! This simple, yet elegant beret is so very French. Placed straight on the crown of the head, this beret makes the perfect topper for a back-to-school outfit. It can also be worn at a jaunty angle like an artiste might wear it . . . and a classic black beret is suitable for all ages. You can add a little tab at the top for a traditional look or embellish the band with a delightful bow or flower. Wool felt is the perfect medium for your beret because it has a wonderful feel and is easy to sew. For a soft mohair look, simply brush your completed hat with sandpaper. This will hide the seams and give a sculpted appearance to your creation.

Sizes: XXS–XL (Baby–Adult)

Skill Level: Beginner

Materials

- ½ yard wool felt
- ½ yard lightweight woven fabric for the lining. The designer used broadcloth. Other possibilities include batiste, gingham, or quilter's cottons.
- OPTIONAL: 150 grit sandpaper for brushing the felt

Cut the Pattern Pieces

From the felt: Cut 1 piece each from the top crown and bottom crown patterns. Cut 1 piece from the band pattern (on a fold). **OPTIONAL:** Cut a ¼" × 1" piece for a top tab. If you are adding the top tab, be sure to make a slit in the position indicated on the top crown pattern.

From the lining fabric: Cut 1 piece each from the top crown and bottom crown patterns.

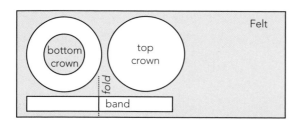

FIGURE 1: Cutting Layout

Assemble the Hat

1 **OPTIONAL:** Insert the tab piece into the slit on the felt top crown. Arrange the tab so that there is a ¼" overhang on the *wrong side* of the top crown piece. Use a hand needle to lightly whipstitch (see chapter 1) the tab in place and close the slit, making sure the stitching does not show on the opposite side. (See Figure 2.)

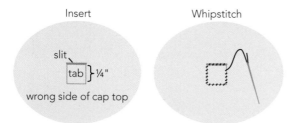

FIGURE 2

2 Place the **felt** top and bottom crown pieces together, right sides facing. Stitch together, ¼" from the aligned *outer* edges. Trim the seam allowance down to ⅛". Repeat the process with the **lining fabric** crown pieces, but leave a 2" opening for turning, and do not trim the seam allowance. (See Figure 3.) Fold the un-sewn lining edges over ¼" to the wrong side and press.

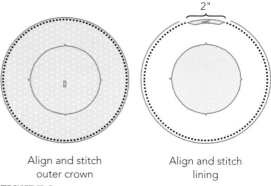

Align and stitch outer crown

Align and stitch lining

FIGURE 3

3 Fold the band piece in half lengthwise, wrong side facing in. Press to make a crease. With the right sides facing, bring the short ends of the band together. Stitch ¼" from the aligned short edges. (See Figure 4.) Press the seam allowance open and turn the band right side facing out.

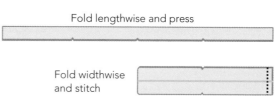

Fold lengthwise and press

Fold widthwise and stitch

FIGURE 4

4 With the felt top/bottom crown assembly still turned wrong side out, slip the band inside the opening in the bottom crown. The right sides should be facing. Align the seam and notches in the band with the notches in the opening and pin together. Align and pin the edges in between. Stitch together, ¼" from the aligned edges. (See Figure 5.)

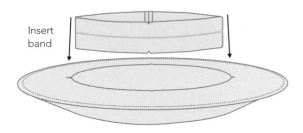

Insert band

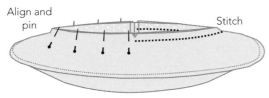

Align and pin

Stitch

FIGURE 5

5 Bring the band up and away from the felt top/ bottom assembly. Turn the lining fabric crown assembly so that the right side is facing out. Slip it inside the band with the right sides facing. Match the notches, align, pin, and stitch as described in the previous step. (See Figure 6.)

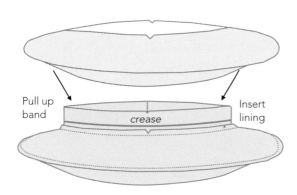

Pull up band

crease

Insert lining

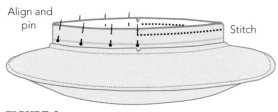

Align and pin

Stitch

FIGURE 6

6 Turn the beret right side out through the opening in the lining fabric crown pieces. Hand or machine stitch the opening closed. Tuck the lining into the felt top/bottom. Arrange the band so that it is folded at the crease and the seam allowances are up against the bottom crown pieces. Pin the outer crown and lining layers together, about a half inch above the seam. Hand or machine stitch at the position of the seam to set the layers together. (See Figure 7.)

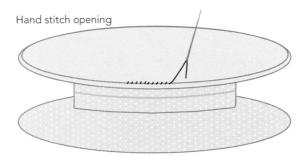

Hand stitch opening

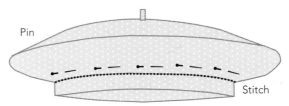

Pin

Stitch

FIGURE 7

7 **OPTIONAL:** For a softer look, "brush" the felt by lightly rubbing it with 150 grit sandpaper. Remove any fuzz balls and smooth the fibers with your hands.

8 **OPTIONAL:** Add an embellishment, like a flower or bow, if desired. (See the appendix for instructions on making embellishments.)

GOING VINTAGE

1920s Hat

1920s HAT

By Bonnie Shaffer (Hats With a Past)

This stylish hat is based on a vintage cloche hat from the Roaring Twenties. Fully lined and topstitched, it has a crisp, couture look that is timeless. The pieced crown has a unique, architectural feel. You can flip the brim up for a ride in a roadster, or turned down to shade your eyes while enjoying a picnic. Instructions are included for adding an attached belt or you can simply tie a jazzy scarf around the band.

Sizes: S–L (Child–Adult)

Skill Level: Beginner/Intermediate

Materials

- **Main fashion fabric:** ¾ yard mediumweight woven fashion fabric. The designer used thick linen for this project. Other possibilities include canvas, corduroy, denim, or home decor fabric.
- **Lining fabric:** ⅝ yard lightweight woven fabric for the lining. The designer used muslin for this project. Other possibilities include batiste, broadcloth, or quilter's cottons.
- OPTIONAL: ⅝ yard lightweight woven fabric for the belt. Possibilities include dupioni, georgette, satin, voile, or any soft cotton solid or print.
- ½ yard heavyweight fusible interfacing (see chapter 1)
- Pinking shears (optional)

Cut the Pattern Pieces

NOTE: All pieces are cut on folds.

From the fashion fabric: Cut 2 pieces from the brim pattern. Cut 1 piece from each of the 4 crown patterns. Cut 1 piece from the band pattern. **NOTE:** Cut the band piece on the bias by making the fold at a 45-degree angle to the selvage edge.

From the lining fabric: Cut 1 piece from each of the 4 crown patterns. Cut 1 piece from the band pattern. **NOTE:** Cut the band piece on the bias by making the fold at a 45-degree angle to the selvage edge.

From the belt fabric (optional): Cut 2 pieces from the band pattern. **NOTE:** Cut the band pieces on the bias by making the folds at a 45-degree angle to the selvage edge.

From the heavyweight fusible interfacing: Cut 1 piece from the brim pattern.

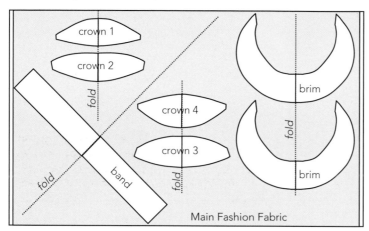

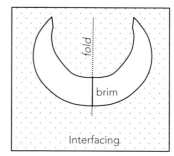

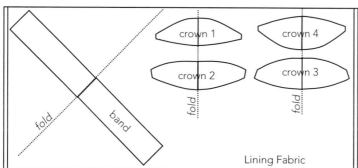

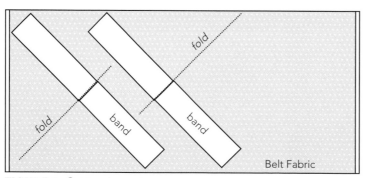

FIGURE 1: Cutting Layout

Assemble the Hat

1 Center the interfacing on the wrong side of one of the brim pieces. There should be a ⅜" distance between the edges all the way around. Fuse according to the manufacturer's instructions.

2 Place outer (fashion fabric) crown piece 1 and outer crown piece 2 together, right sides facing. Align the *single-notched* sides, matching the notches and ends. Stitch ⅜" from the aligned edges. Snip the seam allowance every inch or so and press open. Working on the right side, topstitch ⅛" from each side of the seam. (See Figure 2.)

Align and stitch

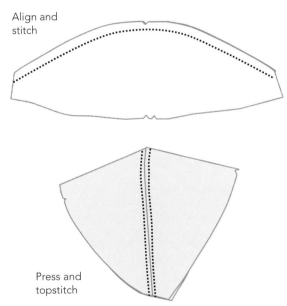

Press and topstitch

FIGURE 2

3 Align the *double-notched* edge of outer crown piece 3 with the corresponding edge of outer crown piece 2, right sides facing. Repeat the stitching, pressing, and topstitching process as described in step 2. (See Figure 3.)

Align and stitch

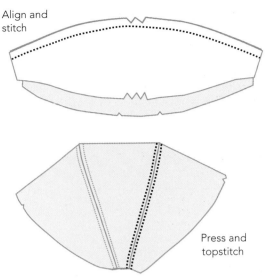

Press and topstitch

FIGURE 3

4 Align the *triple-notched* edge of outer crown piece 4 with that of outer crown piece 3, right sides facing. Repeat the stitching, pressing, and topstitching process as described in step 2. (See Figure 4.)

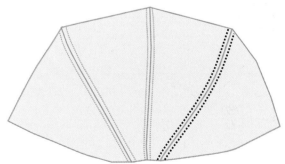

FIGURE 4

5 Fold the outer (fashion fabric) band piece in half widthwise, right side facing in. Stitch ⅜" from the aligned short edges. Press the seam allowance open. With the right sides facing, slip the band over the assembled crown and align the double-notched edges in the front. Match the back seam in the band with the single notch in the back of the crown. Pin, then stitch together, ⅜" from the aligned edges. Pull the band away from the crown, and press the seam allowance open. Topstitch as described for the crown pieces. (See Figure 5.)

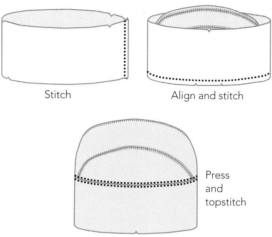

Stitch   Align and stitch

Press and topstitch

FIGURE 5

6 Repeat steps 2–5 with the lining pieces, but eliminate the topstitching steps. Also, when joining the band to the crown (step 5), leave a 4" opening in the back (a 2" open on *each* side of the seam).

7 Place the brim pieces together, right sides facing, and align the edges. Stitch ⅜" from the un-notched *front* brim edge. If you have pinking shears, use them to trim the seam allowance down to ¼", then down to ⅛". Otherwise, snip the seam allowance near the curves, then trim it down to ⅛". Turn the brim so the right side is facing out. Work the edge between your fingers to fully roll out the

seam, then press. Topstitch ⅛" from the *front* edge of the brim. **OPTIONAL:** You can make additional lines of topstitching spaced ¼" apart to add detail to the brim. (See Figure 6.)

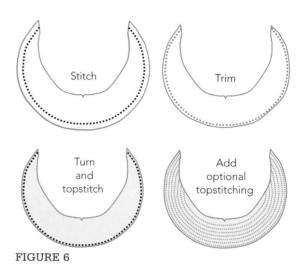

Stitch   Trim

Turn and topstitch   Add optional topstitching

FIGURE 6

8 Place the interfaced side of the brim against the right side of the outer crown assembly and match the single notches in the front. Pin into place. Bring the ends of the brim around to match the notches in the back of the crown and pin. Align and pin the edges in between. Stitch the brim to the crown, ⅜" from the aligned edges. (See Figure 7.)

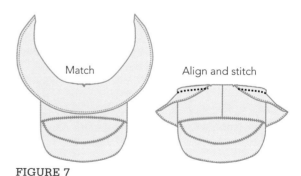

Match   Align and stitch

FIGURE 7

9 Slip the lining over the outer cap, right sides facing, and align the raw edges, making sure the brim is sandwiched in between the layers. Match the notches and seams, and pin together. Stitch ⅜" from the aligned edges. Turn the hat right side out through the opening in the lining. Press the seam all around the base of the hat. Arrange the lining at the opening so that the fold is in line with the stitching. Hand stitch the opening closed. (See Figure 8.)

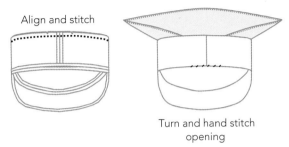

Align and stitch

Turn and hand stitch opening

FIGURE 8

10 **OPTIONAL:** Place the belt pieces together, right sides facing. Stitch ¼" from each of the long edges. Turn right side out and press. Fold in half widthwise with the side that will be on the outside of the finished hat facing in. Stitch the short ends together, ¼" from the aligned edges. Slip the belt over the hat with the raw-edge side facing the hat and align the back seams. Pin into place. **To set the belt into place permanently:** Stitch the layers together at the position of the back seam. Use coordinating thread, and put the stitches "in the ditch" (right in the seam) so they do not show. Hand sew the back layer of the belt into place near the base of the hat. (See Figure 9.)

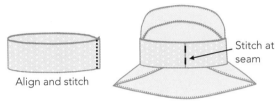

Align and stitch

Stitch at seam

FIGURE 9

Sugar and Spice
Bonnet

SUGAR AND SPICE BONNET

By Jessica Christian (Craftiness Is Not Optional)

This darling little baby bonnet is embellished with a sweet ruffle, because everything is cuter with a ruffle! The amazingly simple design goes together with ease, making for the perfect baby gift. It cinches closed in the back with a soft tie, and you can fasten in a bow underneath a child's adorable cheeks.

Sizes: XXS–XS (Baby–Small toddler)

Skill Level: Beginner

Materials

- **Main fashion fabric:** ⅜ yard light- to mediumweight woven fabric. The designer used quilter's cottons for this project. Other possibilities include batiste, gingham, or seersucker.
- **Ruffle fabric:** ⅛ yard light- to mediumweight woven contrasting fashion fabric. The designer used a quilter's cotton for the ruffle.
- **Lining fabric:** ⅜ yard soft, lightweight woven fabric for the inside of the hat. It should coordinate with the main fashion fabric because it will be visible at the back casing.
- 2 yards of ¾"-wide twill tape (you can substitute soft, satin ribbon, but it is a little trickier to sew)
- Rotary cutter, cutting mat, and clear ruler
- Safety pin (to insert twill tape into casing)

Cut the Pieces to Size

NOTE: This pattern does not include pattern pieces. You will cut the pieces to specific sizes noted below.

From main fashion fabric: Cut a 9" × 17½" rectangle.

From the contrasting lining fabric: Cut a 9" × 17½" rectangle.

From the ruffle fabric: Cut a 3" × 28" strip.

From the twill tape: Cut a 26"-long strip *and* a 43"-long strip.

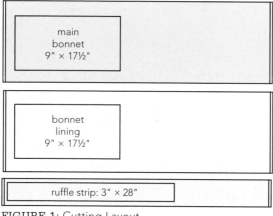

FIGURE 1: Cutting Layout

Assemble the Hat

1 Fold the ruffle strip in half lengthwise, wrong side facing in, and press. Unfold, then fold the long raw edges over to meet at the center crease and press. Run basting stitches through all layers, ¼" from each long raw edge. Pull the loose bobbin threads (on the underside of the fabric) to gather the ruffle to the length of the long edge of the main bonnet piece. (See Figure 2.)

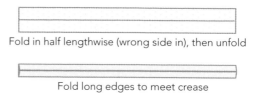

Fold in half lengthwise (wrong side in), then unfold

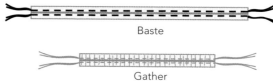

Fold long edges to meet crease

Baste

Gather

FIGURE 2

2 With the wrong side of the ruffle (with raw edges in the center) facing down, place it on the right side of the main bonnet piece with the front edge of the ruffle ½" from the front edge. Pin, then stitch into place, right along the center crease. (See Figure 3.)

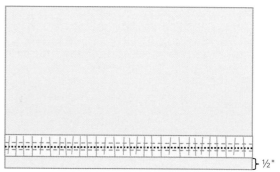

½"

FIGURE 3

3 Place the main bonnet and bonnet lining pieces together, right sides facing. Stitch the layers together, ⅜" from the edges, leaving a 4" opening in the back (opposite the ruffle) edge. Trim the seam allowance at the corners and turn right side out. Work the edges between your fingers to fully roll out the seams. Fold the edges at the opening so they are flush with the back edge and press. (see Figure 4.)

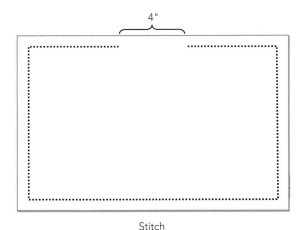

4"

Stitch

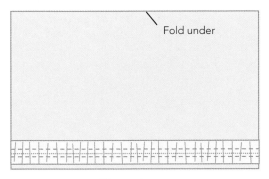

Fold under

Trim and turn

FIGURE 4

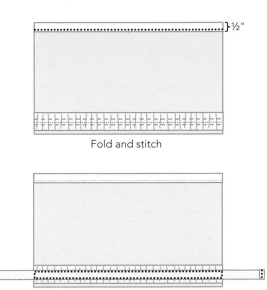

½"

Fold and stitch

Stitch center and ends of tape

FIGURE 5

4 Fold the back edge over to the right side ½" and press. Stitch into place, ⅛" from the edge, to form the casing. Be sure to backstitch at the beginning and end of the stitching. Center the 43" length of twill tape on top of the ruffle and pin into place. Stitch in a rectangular shape, ⅛" from the twill tape edges on the long sides, and ⅛" from the side bonnet edges on the short sides. Fold the ends over ¼" twice, and stitch back and forth over the center of the folds to secure. (See Figure 5.)

5 Fold the 26" piece of twill tape in half lengthwise and press. Fold the ends under ½" to the inside to enclose. Stitch ⅛" from the aligned long edges. Use a safety pin to insert the tape into the casing. Gather the back of the bonnet to the desired tightness, and tie the ends of the tape into a secure knot that a baby can't undo. For extra security, you can stitch the ties into place at the casing ends. (See Figure 6.) Tie the ends into a sweet bow, if you like.

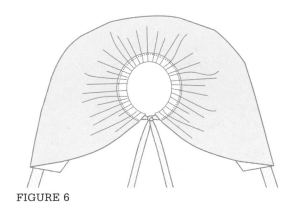

FIGURE 6

Collage Cloche

COLLAGE CLOCHE

By Bari J. Ackerman (Bari J.)

This beautiful hat has the silhouette of a classic cloche, but with a free, artistic twist. The center of the crown is a great place to showcase a gorgeous print. The wool felt side panels give the hat a soft, flexible fit. The focal point of the hat, however, is the face-framing brim. Layered fabric motifs and free-motion stitching (see chapter 1) impart texture, and a unique edge finishing technique completes the multidimensional look.

Sizes: XS–L (Toddler–Adult)

Skill Level: Beginner/Intermediate

Materials

- ¼ yard wool felt for the side panels
- ¼ yard lightweight woven fabric for the crown's center and the brim base. The designer used her line of quilter's cottons for this project. Other possibilities include broadcloth, homespun, or muslin.
- Scraps of fabric with various-sized motifs (you will need approximately 30 motifs)
- ¼ yard woven cotton fusible interfacing (see chapter 1)
- 1 yard of ⅛"-thick cording
- OPTIONAL: New or vintage brooch

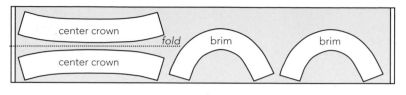

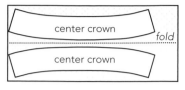

Woven Fabric

Interfacing

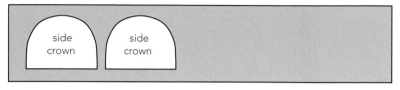

Felt

FIGURE 1: Cutting Layout

Cut the Pattern Pieces

From the felt: Cut 2 pieces from the side crown pattern. **NOTE:** *Before cutting,* you should machine wash and air dry the felt for extra softness and texture.

From the woven fabric: Cut 2 mirror-image pieces from the center crown pattern (near a fold). Cut 2 pieces from the brim pattern.

From the fusible interfacing: Cut 2 mirror-image pieces from the center crown pattern (near a fold).

From the scraps: Cut 30 or so fabric motifs.

Assemble the Hat

1 Following the manufacturer's instructions, apply the fusible interfacing to the wrong side of both center crown pieces.

2 Place the center crown pieces together with the right sides facing and pin. Stitch together, ½" from the double-notched edges. Press the seam allowance open, and topstitch ¼" from *each* side of the seam. (See Figure 2.)

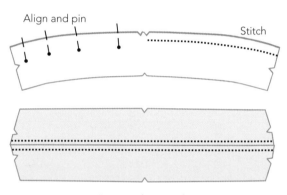

Align and pin

Stitch

Press and topstitch

FIGURE 2

3 With the right sides facing, align one long side of the center crown assembly with the curved edge of a side crown piece. Match the ends and center notches and pin together. Stitch ½" from the aligned edges. Press the seam allowance open, and topstitch ¼" from *each* side of the seam. (See Figure 3.) Repeat with the other side piece to complete the crown.

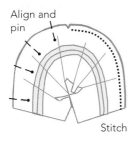

Align and pin

Stitch

Press and topstitch

FIGURE 3

4 Place the 2 brim pieces together, right sides facing. Stitch together, ½" from the aligned short edges. Press the seam allowance open. Lay the fabric motifs on the wrong side of the brim piece fabric. Make sure the edges of the motifs do not extend beyond the outer edge. The motifs may extend beyond the inner edge, however, because you will later trim the edge. Pin each motif into place until the wrong side of the brim fabric is covered. Free-motion sew each motif into place (see chapter 1), removing pins as you go along. NOTE: This is simply doodle stitching . . . be free with it. With fabric collage, you don't need to strive for perfection. If you feel your stitching is too long or too short here and there, simply go back over it. You can doodle leaves, flowers, words, and so on, or just trace the existing motifs. Cut the excess motif fabric from the *inner* edge (if needed, you can use your pattern piece as a guide). Trim the base fabric at the outer edge *around* the motifs. Line up the cording with the outer edges of the motifs. Set your machine to a medium-spaced zigzag stitch that is wide enough to cover the cording. Stitch all around the brim, aligning the cording with the edges as you go. Cut the cording when you reach the start point. (See Figure 4.)

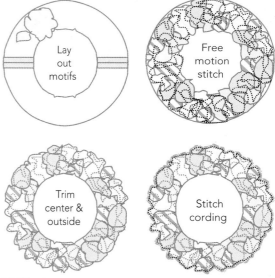

Lay out motifs

Free motion stitch

Trim center & outside

Stitch cording

FIGURE 4

5 With the outer (collaged) side of the brim facing the right side of the crown, match the notches and pin the edges into place. Stitch ½" from the aligned edges. Zigzag or serger finish the seam. Press the seam allowance up against the inside of the crown. Topstitch along the crown, ¼" from the seam. (See Figure 5.)

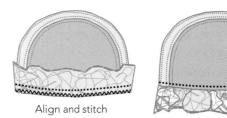

Align and stitch

Press and topstitch

FIGURE 5

6 **OPTIONAL:** Pin a brooch to the crown's front near the brim seam.

Liesl Cloche

LIESL CLOCHE

By Mary Abreu (Confessions of a Craft Addict)

This cloche hat takes you back to an era of sweet innocence. The simple design features a pieced crown and a wonderful curved brim. This modest, yet bold style flatters girls and women of all ages. Sew it up in quilter's cotton or use a special occasion fabric, such as silk shantung or cotton velvet. Get creative and line the brim with a contrasting fabric. And you can embellish the cloche with silk spiderweb roses, ribbon, trim, or some vintage buttons.

Sizes: XXS–L (Baby–Adult)

Skill Level: Beginner/Intermediate

Materials

- **Main fashion fabric:** ½ yard mediumweight woven fashion fabric. The designer used quilter's cottons and canvas for this project. Other possibilities include corduroy, denim, silk, taffeta, twill, or velvet.
- **Lining fabric:** ⅜ yard lightweight woven fabric. The designer used muslin for this project. Other possibilities include batiste, quilter's cottons, or silk.
- ¼ yard mediumweight fusible interfacing (see chapter 1) for the brim.
- OPTIONAL: 1 yard of ribbon or trim to embellish the hat.
- OPTIONAL: Silk spiderweb rose embellishment (see instructions in the appendix).

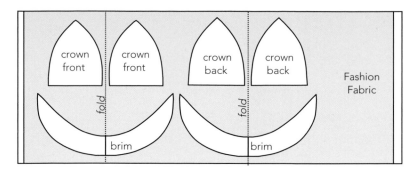
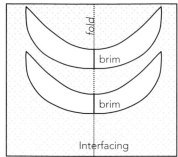

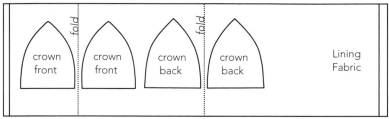

FIGURE 1: Cutting Layout

Cut the Pattern Pieces

From the fashion fabric: Cut 2 mirror-image pieces from the crown front pattern (near folds). Cut 2 mirror-image pieces from the crown back pattern (near folds). Cut 2 pieces from the brim pattern (on fold).

From the lining fabric: Cut 2 mirror-image pieces from the crown front pattern (near folds). Cut 2 mirror-image pieces from the crown back pattern (near folds).

From the fusible interfacing: Cut 2 pieces from the brim pattern (on fold).

Assemble the Hat

1 According to the manufacturer's instructions, fuse the interfacing to the wrong sides of the brim pieces.

2 Place the main fashion fabric **crown front** pieces together, right sides facing, and align the edges. Stitch together, ¼" from the long *single-notched* edges. Press the seam allowance open. Place the main fashion fabric **crown back** pieces together, right sides facing, and align the edges. Stitch together, ¼" from the *triple-notched* edges. Press the seam allowance open. Place the front and back assemblies together, right sides facing, and match the centers and notches. Stitch together, ¼" from the curved side edges. (See Figure 2.) Press the seam allowance open.

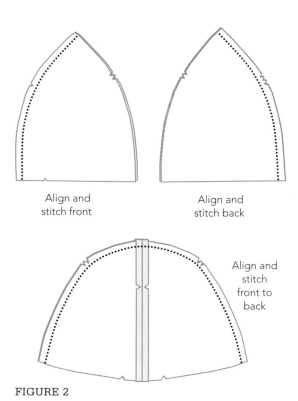

Align and
stitch front

Align and
stitch back

Align and
stitch
front to
back

FIGURE 2

3 Assemble the lining pieces as described in step 2, except leave a 2½" opening in the triple-notched edge, about ½" from the bottom edge. (See Figure 3.)

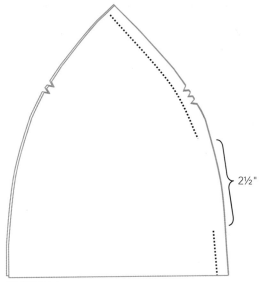

2½"

FIGURE 3

4 Place the brim pieces together, right sides facing. Stitch the layers together, ¼" from the outer (un-notched) edge. Trim the seam allowance down to ⅛". Turn the brim right side out and work the edge between your fingers to fully roll out the seam. Baste stitch the layers together, ⅛" from the aligned inner edges. Topstitch ⅛" from the outer edges. (See Figure 4.)

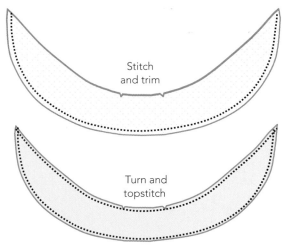

Stitch
and trim

Turn and
topstitch

FIGURE 4

5 With the right sides (the ones that will be on the outside of the finished hat) facing, place the brim on the fashion fabric crown assembly and align the notches in the front. Working towards the back of the hat, align and pin the edges. Stitch together, ⅛" from the aligned edges. (See Figure 5.)

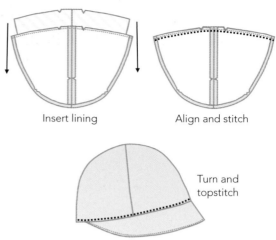

Insert lining   Align and stitch

Turn and topstitch

FIGURE 6

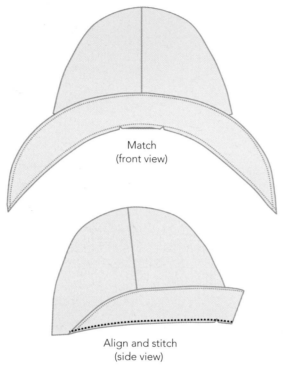

Match
(front view)

Align and stitch
(side view)

FIGURE 5

6 Turn the fashion fabric crown/brim assembly so the wrong side is facing out. Turn the lining so the right side is facing out. Insert the lining into the fashion fabric crown assembly. Make sure the brim is sandwiched in between the layers. Align the raw edges, matching the seams and notches. Stitch together, ¼" from the raw edges. Turn the hat right side out through the opening in the lining. Press the seam at the base of the hat. Topstitch ⅛" from the bottom edge of the crown. (See Figure 6.) Hand stitch the opening closed.

7 **OPTIONAL:** Starting at the back seam, apply the ribbon to the base of the hat by sewing or gluing. Stop stitching/gluing at the starting point. Cut the ribbon about 1" beyond the starting point. Fold it over ½" to the wrong side and stitch or glue into place. **NOTE:** If you are adding a large embellishment like a flower, you can start/stop the ribbon at the attachment point so it is concealed.

8 **OPTIONAL:** Make a silk spiderweb rose as described in the appendix. Attach the finished rose to the cloche.

Heloise Floral Hat

HELOISE FLORAL HAT

By Jennifer Paganelli (Sis Boom)

This wonderful hat pays homage to the flower-adorned hats of the 1950s. What better way to get the look of those stunning (but expensive and delicate) vintage originals than to create one entirely from fabric? The soft flowers are made from bias strips so they hold their shape beautifully and will never fray. The right and wrong sides of the fabric work together to give the flowers a natural, dimensional look. You can use tonal prints in sweet pastels for a muted look, or go with more contrast for some variegation. Definitely a winner of the hit parade, this happy hat is a delightful choice for wonderful sunny days.

Sizes: XS–L (Toddler–Adult)

Skill Level: Beginner/Intermediate

Materials

- **Main fashion fabric:** 1½ yards lightweight fabric (quilter's cotton recommended). The designer used selections from her Sis Boom fabric line for this project. Other possibilities include batiks and broadcloth.
- **Contrasting fashion fabric:** ⅛ yard lightweight woven fabric for the band. The designer used quilter's cottons in this project. Other possibilities include batiks and broadcloth.
- 1½ yards heavyweight fusible interfacing (see chapter 1)
- Rotary cutter, ruler, and cutting mat
- Fabric marker
- Hot glue gun and glue sticks
- 1 package of coordinating ½"-wide double fold bias tape (for inside finishing)

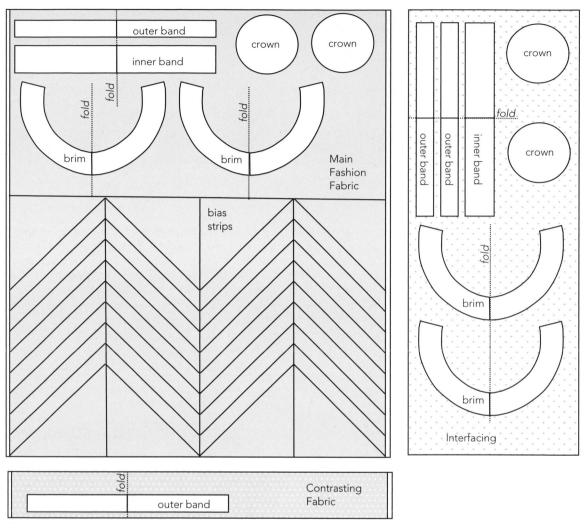

FIGURE 1: Cutting Layout

Cut the Pattern Pieces

From the main fashion fabric: Cut 2 pieces from the crown pattern. Cut 1 piece each from the outer band and inner band patterns (on folds). Cut 2 pieces from the brim pattern (on folds). After cutting out the pattern pieces, cut the remainder of the main fashion fabric into strips for the flowers as follows:

1 Trim away the selvages on both sides (see Figure 2a).

2 Fold the fabric in half widthwise by bringing the trimmed edges together (see Figure 2b).

3 Fold again, so the fabric is now folded into fourths. Cut through all layers at the position of the folds (see Figure 2c).

4 Use a rotary cutter to make 9 cuts (spaced 2¼" apart for sizes XS and S, 2½" for sizes M and L) at a 45-degree angle relative to the edges (see Figure 2d). The resulting 32 bias-cut strips should be 18–19" long measured from point to point.

From the contrasting fashion fabric: Cut 1 piece from the outer band pattern (on a fold).

From the heavyweight fusible interfacing: Cut 2 pieces from the crown pattern. Cut 2 pieces from the outer band pattern, and 1 piece from the inner band pattern (on folds). Cut 2 pieces from the brim pattern (on a fold).

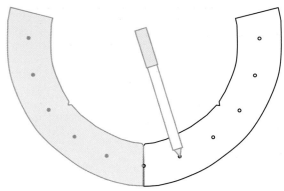

FIGURE 3

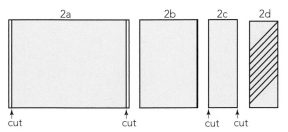

FIGURES 2a–d: Bias Strip Cutting Steps

Assemble the Hat

1 Fuse the heavyweight interfacing to the wrong sides of the band, crown, and brim pieces according to the manufacturer's instructions.

2 Use a nail or a thick needle to pierce the pattern pieces at the positions of the dots. Place the crown pattern atop the right side of 1 crown piece and use your fabric marker to mark the fabric through the holes. Repeat with 1 brim piece and the main fashion fabric outer band piece. NOTE: Because you cut these last 2 pieces on folds, you will need to mark one half, then flip the pattern over and mark the other half. (See Figure 3.)

3 Place the 2 **outer band** pieces together, right sides facing, and align all of the edges. Stitch together, ¼" from one of the notched long edges. Press the seam open. Fold the outer band assembly in half widthwise, right side facing in, and stitch ¼" from the aligned short edges. (See Figure 4.) Press the seam open.

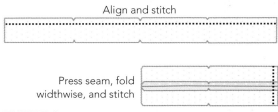

FIGURE 4

4 Fold the **inner band** piece in half widthwise, right side facing in, and stitch ¼" from the aligned short edges. Press the seam open.

5 **For the inner band and inner crown (un-marked) pieces:** With the right sides facing, match the notches and seam of the band with the notches of the crown and pin. Align and pin the edges in between. Stitch the crown to the band, ¼" from the aligned edges. (See Figure 5.) Trim the seam allowance to ⅛".

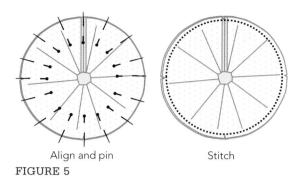

Align and pin   Stitch

FIGURE 5

6 Align, stitch, and trim the outer (marked) crown piece and outer band assembly as described for the inner pieces, making sure the main fabric side of the band is matched with the crown. (See Figure 6.) Turn right side out.

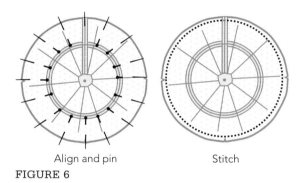

Align and pin   Stitch

FIGURE 6

7 Place the outer hat top over the inner hat top with the wrong sides facing. Match the seams and notches, and align the edges. Stitch the layers together, ⅛" from the aligned edges. (See Figure 7.)

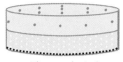

Place hat tops together   Align and stitch

FIGURE 7

8 **For each brim piece:** Align the back edges, right sides facing, and stitch together with a ¼" seam allowance. Press the seam open. Place the brim pieces together, right sides facing. Align the notches. Stitch together ¼" from the *outside* edges. Trim the seam allowance to ⅛". Turn right side out. Work edge between fingers to fully roll out the seam. Press. Topstitch ¼" from outer edge, all the way around the brim. (See Figure 8.)

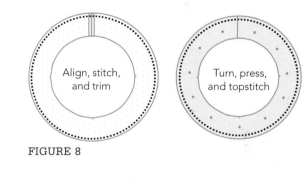

Align, stitch, and trim   Turn, press, and topstitch

FIGURE 8

9 Slip the brim over the crown so that the marked side is facing the right side of the outer crown and the raw edges are in line with those of the crown layers. Match the brim seams with the band seams and pin into place. Match other notches, and align and pin the edges in between. Stitch ¼" from the aligned edges. Finish the edge with the purchased double fold bias tape as described in the "Finishing a Hat with Double Fold Bias Tape" sidebar on page 38. Pull the brim away from the band, and finger press the bias tape up against the inner band. (See Figure 9.)

10 Fold all of the fabric strips in half lengthwise, right side facing in, and press to crease. Unfold and run basting stitches horizontally through the middle of each strip, making sure to leave thread tails (several inches long) at each end. After stitching, refold the strips. **For each flower:** Tie each of the tails into a knot at one end, and trim those threads to about ½" long. Pull the bobbin thread (the loose thread on the underside) at the opposite end to gather, keeping the strip folded. Gather as tightly as possible (but not to the point that the thread breaks). Tie a knot, and trim the ends to about ½" long. (See Figure 10.)

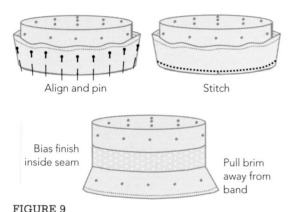

Align and pin   Stitch

Bias finish
inside seam

Pull brim
away from
band

FIGURE 9

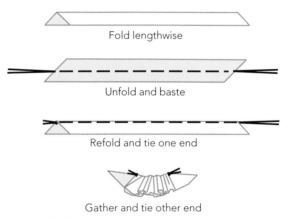

Fold lengthwise

Unfold and baste

Refold and tie one end

Gather and tie other end

FIGURE 10

11 **For each gathered strip:** Coil one of the folded, gathered strips into a circular shape, leaving a small "opening" in the center. Apply a dab of hot glue to the point that is in back, and stick it into place against the back of the flower. Tuck the point that is in the front into the "opening." Pull about ½" of the tip through to the back, and stick into place with a dab of hot glue. Pull the layers apart to fluff the flower. (See Figure 11.)

12 **For each flower:** Apply a spiral of hot glue that is approximately 1" in diameter around a dot on the hat. Place the back of the flower on the glue so the center is just above the dots. (See Figure 12.) Let cool. If the top of the flower feels loose, add a few dabs of glue between the layers of "petals" in the center. Keep in mind each glued flower will look a little different, giving a nice natural look to the hat.

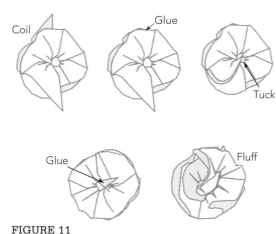

FIGURE 11

 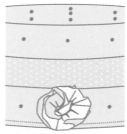

Apply glue   Stick flower into place

FIGURE 12

5

STEPPING OUT

Fantastic Fedora

FANTASTIC FEDORA

By Carla Crim (Scientific Seamstress)

This classic fedora is a stylish way to show off some serious personality without uttering a word. Just watch some old Hollywood films to see fedoras in action—their heartthrob wearers could shoot a gun, kiss a girl, and dance their feet off, never once losing their hat. Even today, sensitive hipsters croon jazzy tunes in funky fedoras. You can make a traditional-looking fedora using wool solids, houndstooth, or tartans. Or, get a little edgy with fun, bold novelty prints (think music notes, flames, or any other retro theme). These great hats aren't just for guys, either. Beautiful starlets wear feminine fedoras to the beach, lunch, and even down the red carpet! Get this softer look by using sweet calicos or lush linens. You can even add a bow or a flower to the band to make a one-of-a-kind statement.

Sizes: XS–XL (Toddler–Adult)

Skill Level: Beginner/Intermediate

Materials

- **Main fashion fabric:** ¾ yard light- to mediumweight woven fabric. The designer used quilter's cottons for this project. Other possibilities include canvas, corduroy, denim, home decor fabric, or wool tartan.
- **Contrasting fashion fabric:** ⅜ yard lightweight woven fashion fabric for the inside of the hat, contrasting belt, and optional bow. Possibilities include quilter's cottons, broadcloth, and gingham.
- 1 yard heavyweight fusible interfacing (see chapter 1)
- ¾ yard fusible fleece (see chapter 1)
- Pencil or fabric marker (does not need to be washable)
- Wash Away™ Wonder Tape or hand needle and thread
- 1 package ½"-wide double fold bias tape
- Spray starch

Cut the Pattern Pieces

From the main fashion fabric: Cut 1 piece from the crown pattern. Cut 1 piece from the outer side band pattern (on a fold). Cut 2 mirror-image pieces from the brim pattern (near a fold). **NOTE:** Cut the brim pattern pieces on the bias by making the fold at a 45-degree angle to the selvage edge.

From the contrasting fashion fabric: Cut 1 piece from the inner side band pattern (on a fold). Cut 1 piece from the crown pattern. Cut 2 pieces from the belt pattern (on a fold). **OPTIONAL:** Cut bow components as described in the Appendix.

From the fusible fleece: Cut 1 piece each from the crown pattern and the outer side band pattern.

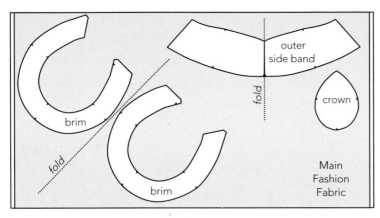

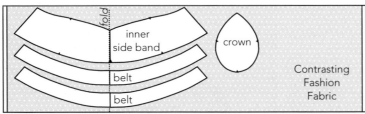

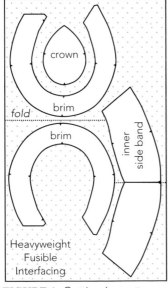

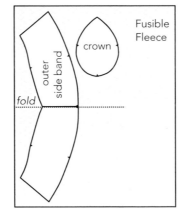

FIGURE 1: Cutting Layout

From the heavyweight fusible interfacing: Cut 2 mirror-image pieces from the brim pattern (near a fold). Cut 1 piece each from the crown pattern and the inner side band pattern (on a fold). After cutting, place the crown interfacing piece atop the crown pattern and trace the dart markings on the right (non-shiny) side.

Assemble the Hat

1 According to the manufacturer's instructions, fuse the fleece to the wrong sides of the outer side band and the main fashion fabric crown piece. According to the manufacturer's instructions, fuse the heavyweight interfacing to the wrong sides of the inner side band, the contrasting fashion fabric crown piece, and both brim pieces.

2 Fold the crown piece that is fused to the heavyweight interfacing in half lengthwise with the right side facing in. Stitch at the position of one of the markings to form a small dart. **For each side band piece:** Fold each piece in half widthwise (right side facing in), bringing the short back edges together. Stitch the back edges together with ¼" seam allowance. (See Figure 2.) Press the seam open.

Fold and stitch dart in crown lining

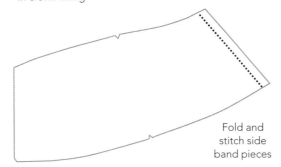

Fold and stitch side band pieces

FIGURE 2

3 **For each side band piece:** Run a row of basting stitches along the top edge from one side notch to the other, ½" from the top edge. Lightly pull the loose bobbin thread (on the underside) to gather. (See Figure 3.)

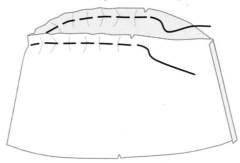

Baste and gather crown top

FIGURE 3

4 **For the outer (fleece-fused) pieces:** With the right sides facing, align the dip in the front of the side band with the notch in the front of the crown piece. Pin together. Match the side notches and pin. Arrange the front side band edges so that they are in line with those of the top, and the gathers are evenly distributed, then pin. Match the point in the back of the crown piece with the seam in the side band and pin. Align and pin the layers between the side notches and back seam. (See Figure 4.)

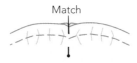

Match

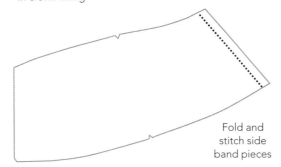

Align and pin front   Align and pin back

FIGURE 4

5 Stitch the crown piece to the side band, ¼" from the aligned edges. Remove the basting stitches. Turn the hat top right side out. Finger press the seam allowance against the side band. Topstitch all around the top of the side band, ⅛" from the seam. Assemble the inner (interfacing-fused) side band and crown pieces as described for the outer pieces, but omit topstitching, and trim the seam allowance to ⅛". **NOTE:** The heavyweight interfacing has a tendency to pucker when stitching around curves. Keep in mind this stitching will be deep inside the hat, and small puckers will not be visible. Place the outer hat top over the inner hat top with the wrong sides facing. Align the seams and notches. Stitch the layers together, ⅛" from the aligned edges. (See Figure 5.)

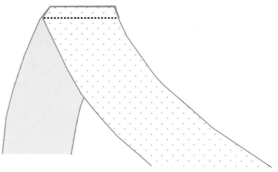

FIGURE 6

7 Stitch ¼" from the outer edge, all the way around the brim. Make a second row of stitching ¼" from the first. Repeat the process until you have 4 (sizes XS–S) or 5 (sizes M–XL) rows of stitching. (See Figure 7.)

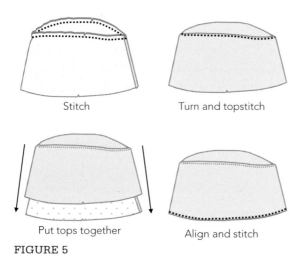

Stitch   Turn and topstitch

Put tops together   Align and stitch

FIGURE 5

6 **For each brim piece:** Align the back edges and stitch together with ¼" seam allowance. Press the seam open. Place the brim pieces together, right sides facing. Align the notches. Stitch together ¼" from the *outside* edges. Trim seam allowance to ⅛". Turn right side out. Work edge between fingers to fully roll out the seam. Press. (See Figure 6.)

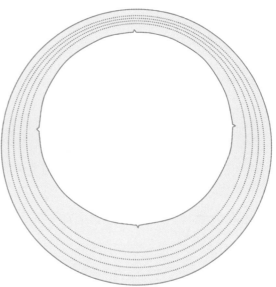

FIGURE 7

8 Slip the brim over the cap top so that the right side (the one that will be on top in the finished hat) is facing the right side of the outer cap and the raw edges are in line with those of the cap layers. Match the notch next to the brim seam with the aligned back side band seam and pin into place. Match the other notches, and align and pin the edges in between. Zigzag stitch over the aligned edges to set them into place. (See Figure 8.)

9 To finish the brim/band edge, apply double fold bias tape as described in the "Finishing a Hat with Double Fold Bias Tape" sidebar on page 38. Topstitch the bias tape in place. Press the brim to remove any bends or wrinkles. For best results, saturate the hat with spray starch before shaping the brim (see chapter 1). Turn the band up in the back, and arrange so the fold is just below the side band/brim seam. Pull the brim to a point in the front. Work the sides of the brim between your fingers so the transition from front to back is smooth. (See Figure 9.)

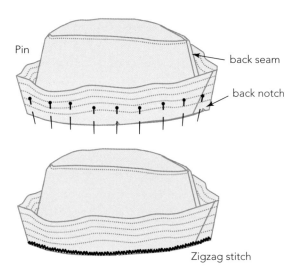

Pin

back seam

back notch

Zigzag stitch

FIGURE 8

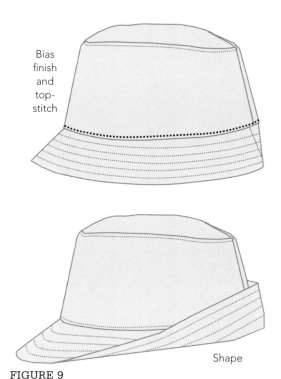

Bias finish and top- stitch

Shape

FIGURE 9

10 Place the belt pieces together, right sides facing. Stitch together, ¼" from the long edges. Turn right side out and press. Zigzag finish the raw ends. Fold the belt in half lengthwise, right side facing in. Stitch ¼" from the short edges. Press the seam allowance open. Slip the belt over the hat and align the back seams. (See Figure 10.) If you want to set the belt permanently in place, tack the belt into position at the back seam. **OPTIONAL:** Add a bow to the side of the belt (see the "Fabric Bow" instructions in the appendix).

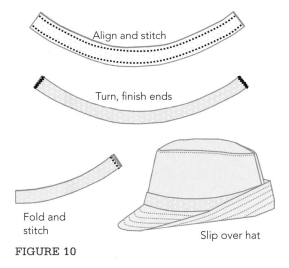

Align and stitch

Turn, finish ends

Fold and stitch

Slip over hat

FIGURE 10

Jackie Pillbox Hat

JACKIE PILLBOX HAT

By Dolin O'Shea (Lulu Bliss)

The pillbox hat was the must-have fashion accessory of the 1960s. Popularized by First Lady Jacqueline Kennedy, this iconic hat remains a couture favorite. From royal weddings to horseraces, this hat is the perfect topper for fancy events. You can go for a demure look with an elegant fabric and a simple embellishment, or take it over the top with feathers, netting, and baubles galore.

Sizes: One size fits all

Skill Level: Beginner/Intermediate

Materials

- **Main fashion fabric:** ¼ yard light- to mediumweight woven fabric. The designer used a wool-blend tweed. Other possibilities include linen, quilter's cottons, or velveteen.
- **Lining fabric:** ¼ yard soft, lightweight woven fabric for the inside of the hat. The designer used silk crepe de chine. Other possibilities include cotton, polyester, or rayon linings.
- ⅝ yard extra firm sew-in interfacing (see chapter 1)
- Fabric marker (does not need to be washable)
- ¼ yard of ⅛"-wide coordinating ribbon for bobby pin loops
- 2 bobby pins
- OPTIONAL EMBELLISHMENTS: The designer used ¾ yard of 1½"-wide grosgrain ribbon for an exterior bow, but feel free to decorate your hat with any sort of ribbon, trim, netting, flowers, buttons, and so on. See the appendix for embellishment ideas and instructions.

Cut the Pattern Pieces

From main fashion fabric: Cut 1 piece from the crown pattern. Cut 1 piece from the band pattern (on a fold).

From lining fabric: Cut 1 piece from the crown pattern. Cut 1 piece from the band pattern (on a fold).

From interfacing: Cut 1 piece from the crown pattern. Cut 1 piece from the band pattern (on a fold).

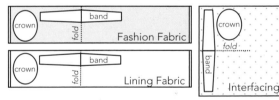

FIGURE 1: Cutting Layout

Assemble the Hat

1 With a fabric marker, draw seam lines on the *interfacing* band and crown pieces, ⅝" from the cut edges. **NOTE:** The marked sides will be referred to as the right sides. With your scissors, clip small "Vs" in the seam allowance all the way around the crown, and along one long edge of the band. Space the "Vs" about ¾" apart, and make sure you do not clip beyond the marked seam lines. (See Figure 2.)

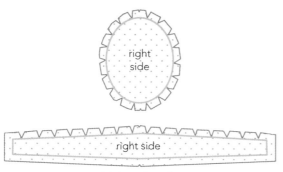

Mark and notch

FIGURE 2

between. Stitch together, ⅝" from the aligned edges. Finger press the seam allowance open. Topstitch ⅛" from *each* side of the seam. Trim the seam allowance down to ¼". Turn right side out and set aside. (See Figure 4.)

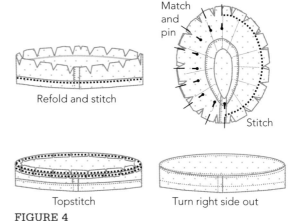

FIGURE 4

2 Fold the other long edge of the band over to the wrong side at the position of the marked line and press to make a crease. Unfold. Fold the band piece in half widthwise, right side facing in. Stitch ⅝" from the aligned short edges. Trim one of the seam allowances down to ⅛". Press the untrimmed seam allowance over the trimmed one and sew through all layers, ½" from the seam. (See Figure 3.)

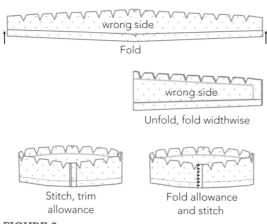

FIGURE 3

3 Refold the bottom edge of the band at the crease. Stitch into place, ½" from the folded edge. With the right sides facing, match the small notches in the interfacing crown piece with the small notch and seam in the top edge of the band. Pin into place, then align and pin the raw edges in

4 Make "Vs" in the *fashion fabric* band and crown pieces as described in step 1. **NOTE:** If you wish to make seam markings, you can draw them on the wrong side of the fashion fabric. Fold the band piece in half widthwise, right side facing in. Stitch ½" from the aligned short edges. Press the seam allowance open. Join the band to the crown as described in step 3. Turn right side out after topstitching and set aside. (See Figure 5.)

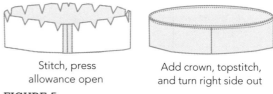

Stitch, press allowance open

Add crown, topstitch, and turn right side out

FIGURE 5

5 Make "Vs" in the *lining fabric* band and crown pieces as described in step 1. **NOTE:** If you wish to make seam markings, you can draw them on the wrong side of the lining. Fold the band piece in half widthwise, right side facing in. Stitch ⅝" from the aligned short edges. Press the seam allowance open. Join the band to the crown as described in step 3. After topstitching, fold the bottom edge over ¾" to the wrong side and press. Set aside without turning. (See Figure 6.)

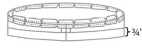

Stitch, press allowance open

Add crown, topstitch, and fold bottom edge

} ¾"

FIGURE 6

6 Slip the exterior hat over the hat form made of interfacing. Make sure the wrong side of the exterior hat is facing the right side of the hat form. Fold the excess raw edge of the exterior hat over the bottom edge of the form and press. Stitch through all layers, ¼" from the bottom edge. (See Figure 7.)

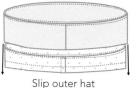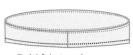

Slip outer hat over form

Fold fabric edge over form and stitch

FIGURE 7

7 Cut the small piece of ribbon into two 4½" lengths. On the exterior hat piece, measure along the inside bottom edge 5" from one side of the band seam, and place a pin to mark. Fold one of the ribbon pieces in half and pin in place against the inside of the hat at the 5" mark. You will want to make sure that the folded end of the ribbon just peeks out from the bottom edge of the hat, no more than ¼". With hand sewing needle and thread, tack both layers of the folded ribbon to the inside of the hat. (See Figure 8.) Repeat the measuring and tacking process on the opposite side.

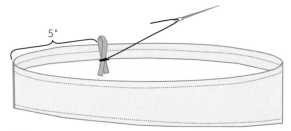

5"

FIGURE 8

8 OPTIONAL: Here is where you get to have a lot of fun decorating your hat! Hand sew any sort of embellishment to the exterior of your hat. Instructions to make a flat grosgrain bow are provided in the "Flat Ribbon Bow" section within the appendix. Keep any visible stitches neat and tidy on the exterior, and make sure you place any knots on the *inside* of the hat.

9 Place the lining inside the exterior hat, wrong sides facing. Align the band seams. Arrange the edges of the lining so that they are in line with the stitching on the exterior band. Pin the layers together. With a hand sewing needle and thread, slip stitch (see chapter 1) the lining into place. (See Figure 9.) If necessary, you can tack the lining to the hat with small back stitches, right along the crown seam. If you do this, make sure your stitches do not show through on the outside.

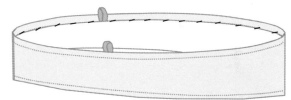

FIGURE 9

DOWNTOWN HAT

By Lisa Carroccio (Domestic Diva's Disasters™)

Here is a hot trend that comes straight from the streets of NYC. If you're looking for a cool hat that will get your dude noticed, this is it. This hat is designed for that bright, mischievous boy who may one day head to Harvard, but no one would ever dare to call him a geek. Based on a cadet-style skateboarding hat, this design features a sturdy brim and lots of double topstitching. Sew it up in denim, twill, wool, or quilter's cotton. You can also make the Downtown Hat for girls and adults, because boys shouldn't have all the fun!

Sizes: XXS–XL (Baby–Adult)

Skill Level: Advanced

Materials

- ⅝ yard of medium- to heavyweight fashion fabric. The designer used denim for this project. Other possibilities include canvas, corduroy, home décor fabrics, twill, or wool.
- ¼" yard (or a 6" × 9" piece) of extra firm double-sided fusible interfacing (see chapter 1)
- OPTIONAL: Universal or jeans single or double needle (size appropriate for fabric thickness)
- OPTIONAL: Button, rivet, or other embellishment, ¼" to 1" diameter

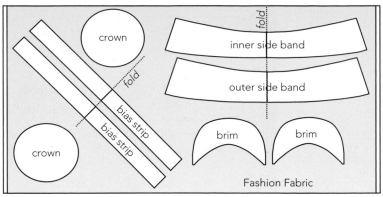

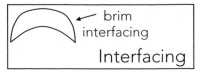

FIGURE 1: Cutting Layout

Cut the Pattern Pieces

From the fashion fabric: Cut 2 pieces from the crown pattern. Cut 1 piece each from the inner and outer side band patterns (on folds). Cut 2 pieces from the brim pattern. Cut 2 pieces from the bias strip patterns (on folds that are at a 45-degree angle relative to the selvage edge).

From the fusible interfacing: Cut 1 piece using the brim interfacing pattern.

Assemble the Hat

NOTE: For all double topstitching steps, you can either use a double needle as described in the "Double Topstitching" section in chapter 1, or you can run 2 single rows of topstitching spaced ⅛" apart.

1 Place the outer brim pieces together, right sides facing, and align the edges. Stitch ¼" from the outer brim edge. Trim the seam allowance down to ⅛". Turn right side out. Work the edge between your fingers to fully roll out the seam and press. Slip the interfacing piece between the brim layers. Arrange the piece so that the inner (shorter) edge is ⅜"–½" from the raw edge of the brim and centered relative to the sides. Press to adhere. Stitch just under ¼" from the notched edge. Double topstitch ¼" from the outer edge of the brim. (See Figure 2.)

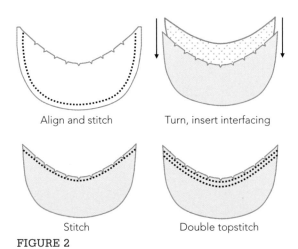

Align and stitch   Turn, insert interfacing

Stitch   Double topstitch

FIGURE 2

2 Fold the single-notched edge of one of the bias strips over ¼" to the wrong side and press. Place the folded strip on the *outer* side band so that the wrong side of the strip is facing the right side of the band, and the centers of the bottom edges (the ones with 9 notches) are in line. Match the ends and the notches, and align the edges in between. For best results, press the strip so it lies flat at the curves. Pin the layers together along the center of the strip. Stitch just under ¼" from the aligned bottom edges. Double topstitch ⅛" from the top folded edge of the bias strip. (See Figure 3.) Press the stitched bias band.

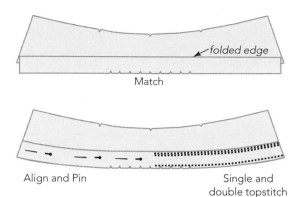

folded edge

Match

Align and Pin

Single and
double topstitch

FIGURE 3

3 With the right (outer) sides facing, align the center of the brim with the center of the outer side band/strip at the 9-notched edge (you should have 4 notches on *each* side of the center notch). Pin together at this position. Match and pin at the positions of the remaining 8 notches. Align the brim with the band/strip all the way to the tips. Arrange the band/strip so that it lies as flat as possible against the brim. It is helpful to let the brim curl a bit inwards into the shape that you will see in the finished cap. With the brim side in contact with the feed dogs, stitch ¼" from the aligned edges. (See Figure 4.)

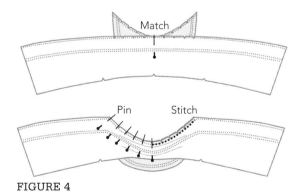

Match

Pin   Stitch

FIGURE 4

4 Pull the band/strip away from the brim and press the seam allowance against the band. Fold the bottom edges of the band over ¼" to the wrong side on *each* side of the brim. Press to set. Fold the outer side band in half widthwise, right side facing in. Unfold the bottom folds near the short ends. Align the short ends, making sure the top folded edges of the band are in line. Stitch together, ¼" from the aligned edges. (See Figure 5.) Press the seam allowance open, then refold the bottom edge.

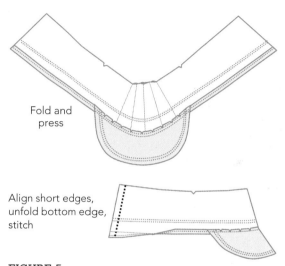

Fold and
press

Align short edges,
unfold bottom edge,
stitch

FIGURE 5

5 Align the edges of the crown with the top edges of the outer band, right sides facing. Match the double notch in the crown with the seam in the band, then match the remaining single notches. Align the edges in between. Stitch together, ¼" from the aligned edges. Turn the hat top so the right side is facing out. Press the seam allowance down against the band. Double topstitch along the band, ⅛" from the seam. (See Figure 6.)

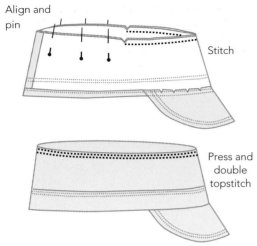

Align and pin

Stitch

Press and double topstitch

FIGURE 6

7 Fold the outer side band in half widthwise, right side facing in. Unfold the bottom folds near the short ends. Align the short ends, making sure the seams are in line. Stitch together, ¼" from the aligned edges. Press the seam allowance open, then refold the bottom edge. (See Figure 8.) Attach the crown as described in step 5, but instead of pressing and topstitching you should simply trim the seam allowance down to ⅛".

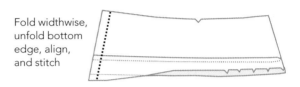

Fold widthwise, unfold bottom edge, align, and stitch

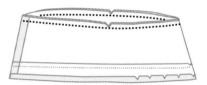

Press seam allowance open, refold edge

FIGURE 8

6 Place the remaining bias strip on the *inner* side band, right sides facing and single-notched edges in line. Match the ends and notches, then align the edges in between. Pin together. Stitch ¼" from the aligned edges. Press the seam allowance down against the inner side band. Fold the 9-notched edge over ¼" to the wrong side and press. (See Figure 7.)

8 With the right sides facing, insert the outer hat top into the inner hat top. Unfold the inner hat top at the front notches. With the brim sandwiched between the hat layers, match and pin at the 9 notches. Align the inner hat edge with the outer hat/brim edges up to the brim tips. Stitch the front together, ¼" from the aligned edges. (See Figure 9.)

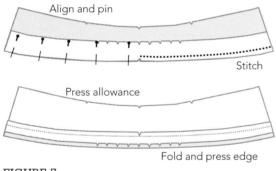

Align and pin

Stitch

Press allowance

Fold and press edge

FIGURE 7

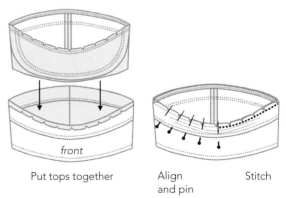

Put tops together

front

Align and pin

Stitch

FIGURE 9

132 • SEWN HATS

9 Pull the hat layers apart, and tuck the inner hat into the outer hat, wrong sides facing. Align the folded bottom edges of the inner and outer bands. Pin the layers together around the perimeter of the hat, including the area above the brim. Double topstitch ⅛" from the bottom edges, all the way around. (See Figure 10.)

10 Pull the inner bias strip down and away from the inside of the cap. Press at the position of the inner band/strip seam. Tuck the inner hat back into the outer hat so the crown pieces are in line and touching. Fold the bias strip over to the inside of the hat. Press around the perimeter to set the fold. (See Figure 11.)

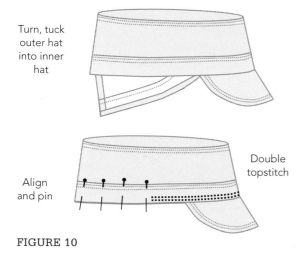

Turn, tuck outer hat into inner hat

Align and pin

Double topstitch

FIGURE 10

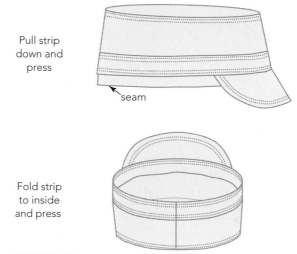

Pull strip down and press

seam

Fold strip to inside and press

FIGURE 11

Raindrop Hat

RAINDROP HAT

By Alexia Marcelle Abegg (Green Bee Patterns)

With its sleek 1960s styling, the Raindrop Hat is mod and functional. The laminated cotton crown will keep your head nice and dry as you hail a cab or splash in the puddles. Water rolls right off the elongated brim, protecting your coif and your peepers. If you have never worked with laminated cotton before, you are going to be pleasantly surprised with how workable it is. There are just a few things to keep in mind. First, *never* place a hot iron directly on the laminated side of the fabric. Press on the back (cotton) side if possible, or use a press cloth as a barrier. Second, an ordinary presser foot works fine when the laminated side is not exposed, but for topstitching you really need a Teflon® or roller presser foot. Finally, pins can leave small holes in the material, so try to position pins in an area like the seam allowance so that holes will not show in the finished hat.

Sizes: XXS–L (Baby–Adult)

Skill Level: Intermediate

Materials

- **Outer fabric:** ½ yard laminated cotton for the outer fabric. The designer used laminated cotton from Free Spirit Fabrics for this project.
- **Lining fabric:** ½ yard light- to mediumweight woven fabric. The designer used quilter's cotton for this project. Other possibilities include batiste, broadcloth, or gingham.
- 1 yard heavyweight fusible interfacing (see chapter 1)
- Teflon® or roller foot for sewing machine

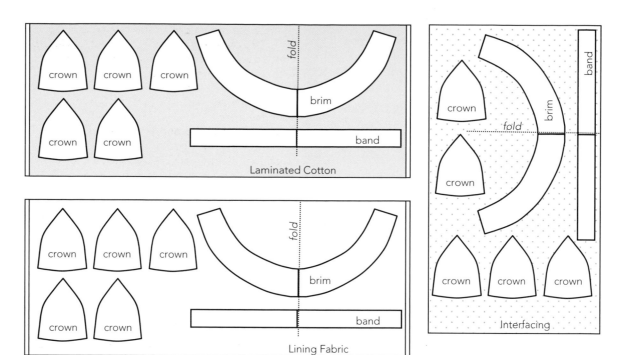

FIGURE 1: Cutting Layout

Cut the Pattern Pieces

From the outer (laminated cotton) fabric: Cut 5 pieces from the crown pattern. Cut 1 piece each from the band and the brim patterns (on folds).

From the lining fabric: Cut 5 pieces from the crown pattern. Cut 1 piece each from the band and the brim patterns (on folds).

From the interfacing: Cut 5 pieces from the crown pattern. Cut 1 piece each from the band and the brim patterns (on folds).

Assemble the Hat

1 Fuse the interfacing to the wrong side of all outer pieces following the manufacturer's instructions. Transfer the dots on the crown pattern to the wrong sides of the outer and lining crown pieces.

2 Fold the *outer* brim piece in half widthwise, right side facing in. Stitch together, ½" from the aligned short edges. Press the seam allowance open. Repeat with the *lining* brim piece. Place the brim pieces together, right sides facing, and align the bottom (wider) edge. Match the notches and the seams, and pin together with lots of pins to prevent shifting during sewing. Stitch ¼" from the aligned bottom edges. (See Figure 2.) Snip the seam allowance.

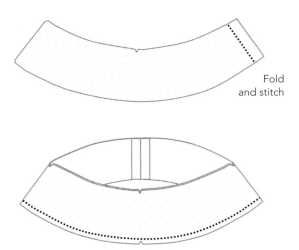

Fold
and stitch

Align and stitch

FIGURE 2

3 Turn the brim right side out. Work the bottom edge between your fingers to fully roll out the seam. Press so that the brim is flat and the top edges are in line. Pin the layers together near the top edge. Topstitch ⅛" from the bottom edge. Make three more rows of topstitching, each ⅜" away from the previous line of stitching. Stitch the layers together about ⅛" from the top edge using a long, loose basting stitch. (See Figure 3.)

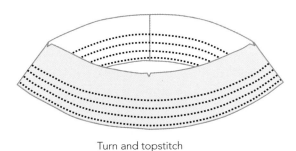

Turn and topstitch

Align and baste stitch

FIGURE 3

4 Fold the *outer* band piece in half widthwise, right side facing in. Stitch ½" from the aligned short edges. Press the seam allowance open. Repeat with the *lining* band piece. Slip the outer band over the brim with the outer right sides facing and the edges with three notches each in line. Match the notches and seams and pin at these positions. Align and pin the edges in between. If needed, gently stretch the brim to accommodate the band. Stitch together, ¼" from the aligned edges. (See Figure 4.)

Fold and stitch

Align and pin   Stitch

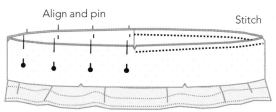

FIGURE 4

5 Flip the brim so the lining side is facing out, and the outer band is on the inside. Slip the outer band over the brim with the outer right sides facing and the edges with three notches each in line. Match the notches and seams and pin at these positions. Align and pin the edges in between. Stitch together, ½" from the aligned edges. Pin the band lining to the brim lining in the center of the band, all the way around the hat. Pull the outer brim up and away from the hat. (See Figure 5.)

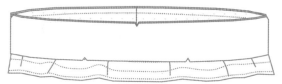

Flip brim, slip band over lining side

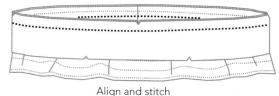

Align and stitch

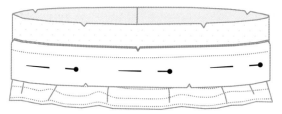

Pin lining pieces, pull outer band up

FIGURE 5

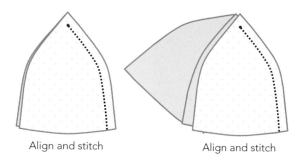

Align and stitch   Align and stitch

Stitch to complete dome

FIGURE 6

6 Place 2 of the *outer* crown pieces together, right sides facing. Using a ½" seam allowance, stitch from the dot to the bottom edge. Be sure to backstitch at the beginning and end of the stitching. Repeat to add a third crown piece to the pair. Continue adding the outer crown pieces until all 5 pieces are sewn together, including the final seam to create a dome shape. (See Figure 6.) Trim the seam allowances down to ⅛". Repeat the assembly process with the crown *lining* pieces, but instead of trimming, snip the seam allowances at the curves and press open.

7 Turn the outer crown so the right side is facing out. With the wrong sides facing, insert the crown lining into the outer crown. Align the bottom raw edges, matching the seams. Stitch together, ¼" from the edge, using a long, loose basting stitch. Snip the bottom edge up to the stitching. Hand tack the outer crown center to the lining crown center. Be sure to put the stitches in the seam so they are not visible on the outside. Working on the outer side of the crown, topstitch ⅛" from the right and left sides of each seam. (See Figure 7.)

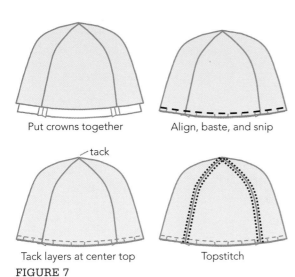

Put crowns together

Align, baste, and snip

tack

Tack layers at center top

Topstitch

FIGURE 7

8 With the right (outer) sides facing, insert the crown into the outer band and align the raw edges. Match the seam and notches in the band with the seams in the crown and pin. Align the edges in between, stretching the snipped crown edge as needed. Stitch together, ¼" from the edge using a long, loose basting stitch. Run a second row of stitching, this time using a regular stitch length, ½" from the edge. (See Figure 8.)

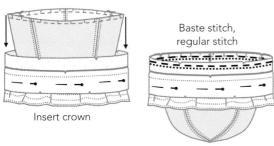

Insert crown

Baste stitch, regular stitch

FIGURE 8

9 With the pins still in place, pull the crown up and away from the outer band. Turn the hat right side out. Working on the *outer* side of the hat, topstitch along the outer band, ⅛" from the band/brim seam. Run a second row of stitching ⅛" from the first. (See Figure 9.)

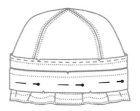

Pull crown up and away from band

Turn and topstitch

FIGURE 9

10 Finger press the band/crown seam allowance against the band. Working on the *outer* side of the hat, topstitch along the outer band, ⅛" from the band/crown seam. Run a second row of stitching ⅛" from the first. Turn the hat lining side out and remove the pins. Fold the raw edge of the band lining over ½" to the wrong side. Bring the folded edge of the band lining up to meet the band/crown seam. Hand stitch into place, arranging the fold as needed to line up with the stitching. (See Figure 10.)

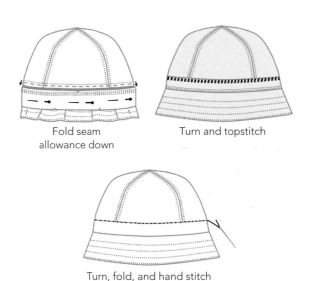

Fold seam allowance down

Turn and topstitch

Turn, fold, and hand stitch lining band

FIGURE 10

Delmar Driving Cap

DELMAR DRIVING CAP

By Carla Crim (Scientific Seamstress)

This driving cap, also known as a flat cap or ivy cap, is pure class on and off the motorway. The versatile design is suitable for use with a range of fabrics. For a traditional, gentlemanly look, go with wool tweeds or tartans. If you prefer a bit cooler cap, try quilter's cottons in bold prints and colors. The provided patterns will make caps scaled for the wee ones, but oversized caps make great photo props (and will fit a child perfectly down the road as he or she grows older).

Sizes: XXS–XL (Baby–Adult)

Skill Level: Advanced

Materials

- **Main fashion fabric:** ⅜ yard light- to mediumweight woven fashion fabric. The designer used quilter's cottons for this project. Other possibilities include canvas, corduroy, denim, home decor fabric, or wool.
- **Lining fabric:** ⅜ yard lightweight woven lining fabric. The designer used muslin for this project. Other possibilities include broadcloth, gingham, quilter's cottons, or synthetic lining material.
- ¼ yard (or 1 package) of InnerFuse™ extra-firm double-sided fusible interfacing (see chapter 1)
- 1 package ½"-wide double fold bias tape
- Washable fabric marker
- OPTIONAL: two ¼"- to ⅜"-wide snaps (press-on or sew-on)
- OPTIONAL: Sewing needle and coordinating thread if using snaps

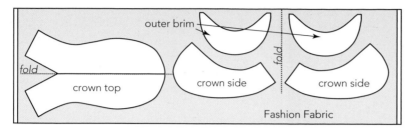

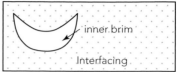

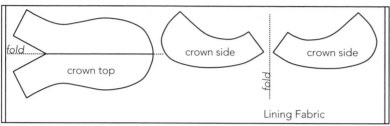

FIGURE 1: Cutting Layout

Cut the Pattern Pieces

From the fashion fabric: Cut 2 pieces from the outer brim pattern. Cut 2 mirror-image pieces from the crown side pattern (near fold). Cut 1 piece from the crown top pattern (on fold).

From the lining fabric: Cut 2 mirror-image pieces from the crown side pattern (near fold). Cut 1 piece from the crown top pattern (on fold).

From the extra-firm double-sided fusible interfacing: Cut 1 piece from the inner brim pattern.

Assemble the Hat

1 If you are planning to tack the brim into place, use your washable marker to mark the dots on the right side of the crown side *lining* fabric pieces. **OPTIONAL:** If you are adding snaps, mark the dots on the right side of the crown side *fashion* fabric pieces and the right side of one of the *outer* brim pieces. Sew or press the snaps into place at the positions of the dots. You should sew the male snaps to the crown and the female snaps to the brim. Make sure the working sides of the snaps are on the right side of the fabric.

2 Fold the fashion fabric **crown top** in half lengthwise, right side facing in. Starting at the back end, stitch ¼" from the *dart edge*. Backstitch when you reach the fold. Snip the seam allowance at the position of the fold, and press open. Place the 2 fashion fabric **crown side** pieces together, right sides facing. Stitch together, ¼" from the short straight front edges. Press the seam allowance open. (See Figure 2.)

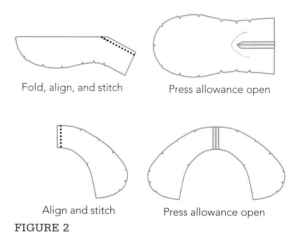

Fold, align, and stitch   Press allowance open

Align and stitch   Press allowance open

FIGURE 2

3 Lay out the crown side assembly with the right side facing up. Place the crown center atop the side assembly with the right side facing down. Match the center front notch in the crown center with the seam in the side assembly. Pin together. Match and pin the adjacent notches, working towards the back corners. Align and pin the edges in between. Stitch the crown top to the crown sides, ¼" from the aligned edges. Stitch slowly, taking care to keep the edges in line and avoid puckering. Press the seam allowances open. Working on the right side of the cap, topstitch ⅛" from *both* sides of the seam. (See Figure 3.)

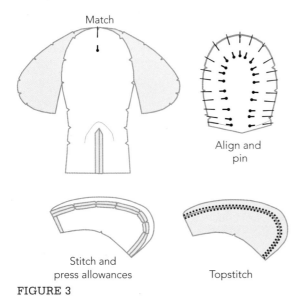

FIGURE 3

Match

Align and pin

Stitch and press allowances

Topstitch

4 Repeat step 2 with the *lining* pieces, but trim seam allowances down to ⅛" rather than pressing and topstitching. With the fashion fabric crown turned right side out, slip the lining inside, wrong sides facing. Match the seams and notches and pin together. Align the edges in between. Stitch the layers together, ⅛" from the aligned edges. (See Figure 4.)

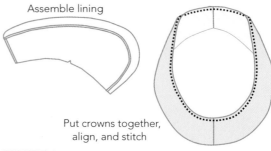

Assemble lining

Put crowns together, align, and stitch

FIGURE 4

5 Place the *outer brim* pieces together, right sides facing, and align the edges. Stitch ¼" from the un-notched front brim edge. Trim the seam allowance down to ⅛". Turn right side out. Work the edge between your fingers to fully roll out the seam and press. Insert the inner brim piece so that the front edges are sitting on top of the seam allowance. Work the back edges up so that they are in line with the inner brim on both sides. Press to set. Topstitch ⅛" from the front edge of the brim. (See Figure 5.)

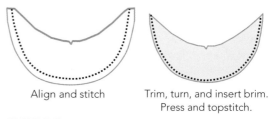

Align and stitch

Trim, turn, and insert brim. Press and topstitch.

FIGURE 5

6 Turn the crown so the lining side is facing out. Place the brim inside the hat and match the notch in the brim with the center front seam of the crown. The top (the one that has snaps on it, if applicable) side of the brim should be facing the right fashion fabric side of the crown. Align and pin the adjacent edges. Stitch the brim to the crown, ¼" from the aligned edges. If you are using the tacking method to attach the crown to the cap, now is a good time to do it. Use a hand needle to sew both layers of the crown to the top side of the brim at the position of the dots. (See Figure 6.) *Make sure the stitching does not go through to the underside of the brim.*

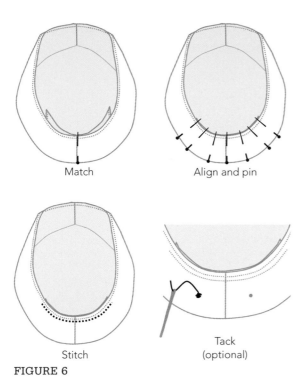

Match

Align and pin

Stitch

Tack
(optional)

FIGURE 6

align the raw edges. Pin into place near the center back dart. Start stitching the tape into place ¼" from the edges, aligning the tape with brim and band edges as you go. When you reach the original fold, stitch over it by ¼", then backstitch. Cut the tape at the end of the stitching end. Turn the cap so the right side is facing out. Refold the tape over the seam allowance. The folded end should neatly overlap the raw end. Turn the cap right side out and arrange the folded edge of the tape so it is in line with the stitching. Secure with pins or basting tape at the position of the brim. Stitch through all layers, ⅛" from the folded edge. Fold the encased edge over to the lining side at the side and back crown edges. Press to set. (See Figure 7.)

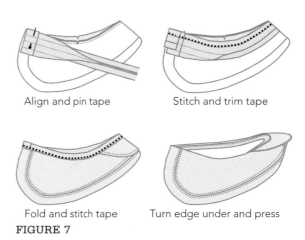

Align and pin tape

Stitch and trim tape

Fold and stitch tape

Turn edge under and press

FIGURE 7

7 Cut a piece of double fold bias tape that is a few inches longer than the perimeter of the opening edge, or just work from the carded tape. Cut the tape so the end is nice and straight, then unfold a few inches. Fold the end over ½" to the wrong (inner) side and press. Place the right side of the tape against the lining side of the crown, and

Mini Top Hat

MINI TOP HAT

By Heather Niziolek (Goosie Girl) and Carla Crim (Scientific Seamstress)

You can put on the ritz with this super-swanky mini top hat. At only 3½" tall, this petite chapeau makes a big statement. The hat is pieced from fleece-fused fabric, and it features an inner foam core that is sturdy, yet lightweight. It goes together quickly, so you can get to the fun part . . . the embellishments! For a sophisticated night on the town, add billowy feathers and glitzy rhinestones. A glammed-out theme hat is also a great way to top off a costume or add holiday spirit to any outfit. These hats are wonderful for children as well. Little girls love them for dress-up and party time, and they make great props for a baby's first photo shoot.

Sizes: One size fits all

Skill Level: Beginner/Intermediate

Materials

- ¼ yard light- to mediumweight woven fashion fabric. The designer used quilter's cottons and sateen for this project. Other possibilities include broadcloth, linen, satins, silks, or wool.
- ⅜ yard fusible fleece (see chapter 1)
- One 9" × 12" sheet of 2mm craft foam
- Hot glue gun and glue sticks
- Appropriately sized clip(s), comb, or headband. For adults with thick hair, a single large spring barrette (70–80mm) or a comb will work well. Alligator clips are better for young children (use 2 for extra hold). For babies and toddlers, elasticized headbands are a good choice.

Optional embellishments: Mix and match from the following categories:

- **Band:** A decoration that goes around the base of the hat, usually trim or ribbon. Gimp (braided ornamental trim) and ruffled fold-over elastic work well.
- **Height:** A tall element like spikes of tulle, feathers, thin leaves, or wiry pieces of garland.
- **Volume:** Something wide and voluminous like a pouf of lace or tulle, or a 3–4" piece of feather boa rolled into a ball.
- **Mass:** Something that will provide weight and a focal point. Suggestions include brooches, bows, silk flowers, fabric rosettes, or themed trinkets.
- **Extras:** Small elements like buttons, gems, or pearls. Veiling also may be added to the underside of the brim.

Assemble the Hat

1 Fuse the fleece to the wrong side of the fashion fabric pieces according to the manufacturer's instructions. Cut a "+" shape on only 1 of the brim pieces, as indicated on the pattern.

2 Fold the bottom un-notched edge of the outer **side band** piece over ½" to the wrong side. Press, then stitch into place, ⅛" from the folded edge. Fold the side band piece in half widthwise, right side facing in. Stitch ¼" from the aligned short edges. (See Figure 2.) Press the seam allowance open.

Cut the Pattern Pieces

From the fashion fabric: Cut 1 piece from the outer side band pattern. Cut 1 piece from the top pattern. Cut 2 pieces from the brim pattern.

From the fusible fleece: Cut 1 piece from the outer side band pattern. Cut 1 piece from the top pattern. Cut 2 pieces from the brim pattern.

From the craft foam: Cut 1 piece from the form side pattern. Cut 1 piece from the form base pattern.

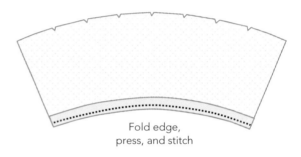

Fold edge,
press, and stitch

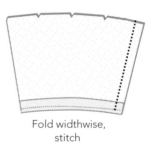

Fold widthwise,
stitch

FIGURE 2

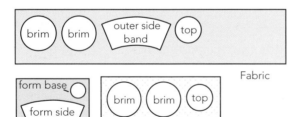

FIGURE 1: Cutting Layout

3 With the right sides facing, match the notches and seam along the top edge of the outer side band piece with the notches in the top piece. Pin together. Using tight, small stitches, sew ¼" from the aligned edges. Trim the seam allowance down to ⅛". Turn the side/top assembly right side out. Work the edge between your fingers to fully turn out the seam. (See Figure 3.)

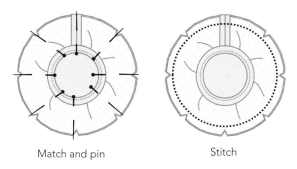

Match and pin   Stitch

Turn

FIGURE 3

4 Place the brim pieces together, right fashion fabric sides facing, and align the edges. Using tight, small stitches, sew ¼" from the aligned edges. Trim the seam allowance down to ⅛". Turn the brim right side out. Work the edge between your fingers to fully turn out the seam. Press the tabs back against the fashion fabric at the center "+". Apply hot glue to the exposed fleece in the center, and carefully push the tabs back into place. (See Figure 4.)

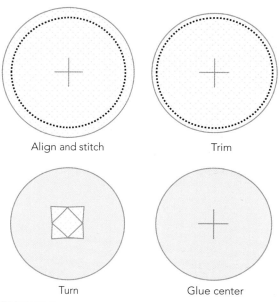

Align and stitch   Trim

Turn   Glue center

FIGURE 4

5 Apply a thin line of hot glue to one short edge of the form side foam. Bring the other short end over and overlap by ¼". Fold the form at the wide end and insert it into the hat top assembly. Arrange it so the overlap is in line with the seam allowance, and the narrow end is about ¼" below the folded edge of the hat top. When viewed from above, it should be as round as possible. Place the form base atop the form side to make sure it fits inside the hat top. Trim slightly, if needed. Once you have a good fit, apply a thin line of hot glue to the narrow end of the form. *NOTE: Try to avoid getting glue on the outside of the hat top, but don't worry if a bit of glue drips inside the form.* Carefully stick the form base into place on top of the form side. Arrange it so the edges of the hat top just cover the form base. (See Figure 5.)

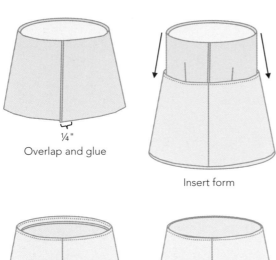

¼"

Overlap and glue

Insert form

Push into place

Add form base

FIGURE 5

6 Apply a 1" diameter circle of glue over the "+" on the brim. Stick the hat base into place at this position, making sure it is perfectly centered. (See Figure 6.) Let cool. Working in small sections, apply glue to the outer perimeter of the hat base, and stick to the brim. Try to avoid getting glue blobs on the brim beyond the position of the base.

brim

Apply glue

top

Stick top into place

FIGURE 6

Embellishment

NOTE: When embellishing, think of the embellishments as "layers" with the taller embellishments being at the back so they will not cover the shorter ones. I like to think of the embellishments as making the visual presence of the hat larger. A plain mini top hat would be just that, plain. Think of your embellishments as a way to expand the hat—and not just "decorate" it. Embellishments, when done properly, will seem to be a part of the hat itself.

7 Wrap the ribbon around the base of the top hat and hot glue or sew into place. If you are adding other embellishments that will cover the ribbon ends, place them at the appropriate place. Otherwise, position the ends at the seam, and neatly fold the ribbon end to cover the start point. Attach the "height" embellishments to the side of the hat. Secure the "volume" embellishment to the base in front of the height elements. Position the "mass" as desired over the volume embellishments. Hot glue or sew the "extras" into place around the arrangement you have created. (See Figure 7.)

Add band

Add height

Add volume and mass

Add extras

FIGURE 7

8 Glue or sew the clip(s), comb, or headband to the underside of the hat.

WORKING AND PLAYING

Sweetie Pie
Chef's Hat

SWEETIE PIE CHEF'S HAT

By Melissa Stramel (Lilac Lane)

This darling chef's hat features a soft, stretchy ribbed-knit band and a poufy woven top. It is reversible, so you can show off two different flavors of fabric. You can use fun novelty prints or go with classic white for the traditional chef's toque. Both child and adult sizes are included, so you can whip up a pair for a mommy-and-me baking day. This pattern is also great for concocting stylish muffin hats. Mix fashion fabrics with cute embellishments, and you'll have a yummy accessory for going out on the town.

Sizes: XS/S and M/L (Toddler and Adult)

Skill Level: Beginner

Materials

- 2 woven fabrics for the reversible crown. For the child's size, you will need ½ yard of each. For the adult's size, you will need ⅝ yard of each. The designer used quilter's cottons for this project. Other possibilities include batiks, broadcloth, or muslins.
- ¼ yard ribbed knit fabric for the band
- Ball-point needle for sewing ribbed knit band

Cut the Pattern Pieces

From woven fabric 1: Cut 1 piece from the crown pattern.

From woven fabric 2: Cut 1 piece from the crown pattern.

From the knit fabric: Cut 1 piece from the band pattern (on a fold).

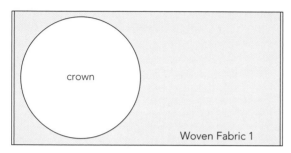

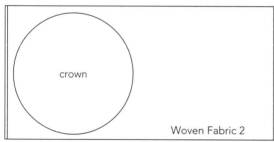

FIGURE 1: Cutting Layout

Assemble the Hat

1 Fold the band piece in half widthwise, right side facing in. Stitch ½" from the aligned short edges. Press the seam allowance open. Fold the band in half lengthwise, wrong side facing in. Stitch ¼" from the aligned edges to hold them together during subsequent steps. (See Figure 2.)

Stitch   Fold and stitch

FIGURE 2

2 For each crown piece: Run a row of basting stitches ⅛" from the edge. Run a second row of basting stitches ¾" from the edge. Pull the loose bobbin threads (on the underside) to gather loosely. *NOTE: You should gather the edge of the crown to a circumference that is a bit larger than that of the band because the knit fabric will stretch.* Evenly distribute the gathers. (See Figure 3.)

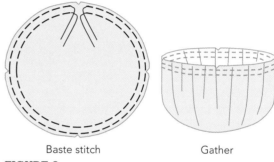

Baste stitch   Gather

FIGURE 3

3 Slip the band loop over one gathered crown piece, right sides facing, and align the edges. Stitch together, ½" from the edges. Turn so the wrong side of the crown piece is facing out. (See Figure 4.)

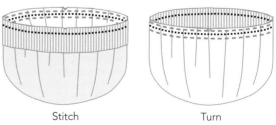

Stitch   Turn

FIGURE 4

4 Slip the second gathered crown piece inside the first crown piece, right sides facing. Make sure you sandwich the band in between the two crown layers. Align the edges and pin. Stitch ½" from the aligned edges, leaving a 3" opening flanking the back seam in the band. (See Figure 5.)

5 Turn the hat right side out through the opening. Slip stitch the opening closed. (See Figure 6.)

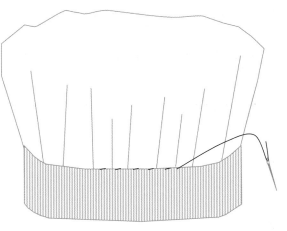

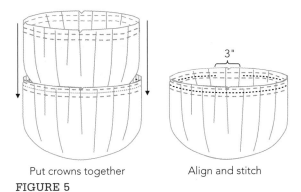

Put crowns together   Align and stitch

FIGURE 5

Turn and hand stitch

FIGURE 6

Hitch and Pitch
Cap

HITCH AND PITCH CAP

By Carla Crim (Scientific Seamstress)

Truckers and baseball players alike know the importance of a great cap. The trim fit allows for maximum speed when rounding corners and barreling down straight runs. The durable brim not only shades your eyes, but also makes you look focused and cool. Use a single favorite fabric, or mix and match prints for a funky look. You can even support your favorite team by loading up with their colors and motifs. The flat front is perfect for personalization with appliqué or embroidery. With three different closure options, this sporty style is perfect (and adjustable) for all ages and sizes.

Sizes: XXS–XL (Baby–Adult)

Skill Level: Advanced

Materials

- ½ yard light- to mediumweight woven fashion fabric. The designer used canvas for this project. Other possibilities include canvas, corduroy, denim, home decor fabric, or quilter's cottons.
- ¾ yard fusible tricot interfacing (see chapter 1)—you can omit if you are using a thicker fashion fabric with a crisp hand
- ¼ yard (or 1 package) of extra-firm double-sided fusible interfacing (see chapter 1)
- 1 package basting tape, such as Wash Away™ Wonder Tape (see chapter 1)
- 1 package ½"-wide single fold bias tape
- Glue stick (see chapter 1)
- ½" covered button kit
- OPTIONAL: Spray starch (for a stiffer cap)
- Back strap notions (choose 1 from list below and refer to table for cutting measurements):
    - ½"-wide hook-and-loop tape (can purchase larger width and trim down)
    - ½"-wide elastic
    - ¾" vest buckle

Cut the Pattern Pieces

From the fashion fabric: Cut 2 pieces from the cap band pattern (on folds). Cut 2 mirror-image pieces from *each* of the following patterns (near folds): cap front, cap side, and cap back. Cut 2 pieces from the outer brim pattern. Also cut the needed back strap strips. (See the table.)

From the fusible tricot interfacing: Cut 2 mirror-image pieces from *each* of the following patterns

(near folds): cap front, cap side, and cap back. Cut 2 pieces from the outer brim pattern.

From the extra-firm double-sided fusible interfacing: Cut 1 piece from the inner brim pattern.

Back Strap Components: Cut the back strap components (hook-and-loop tape or elastic) from leftover fashion fabric to the dimensions given in the table, if applicable.

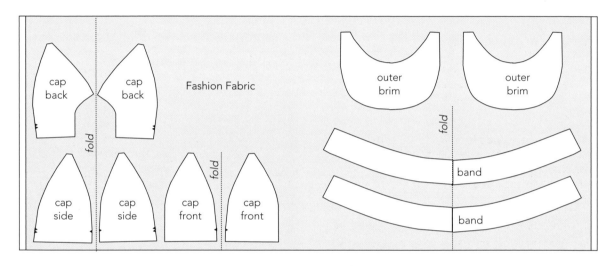

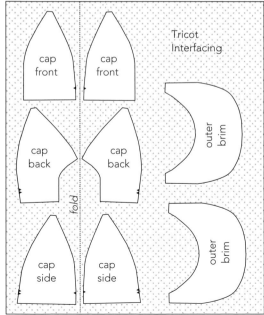

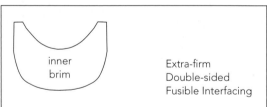

FIGURE 1: Cutting Layout

Size	Hook-and-Loop Tape Back Straps	Elastic Back Strap	Buckled Back Straps
XXS-XS	Cut **2** 8½" x 1¼" strips fabric Cut **1 each** 4" x ½" hook-and-loop tape	Cut **1** 6" x 1¾" strip fabric Cut **1** 4" piece of ½" elastic	Cut **1** 5" x 1¾" strip fabric Cut **1** 4" x 1¾" strip fabric
S-M	Cut **2** 9½" x 1¼" strips fabric Cut **1 each** 4½" x ½" hook-and-loop tape	Cut **1** 7" x 1¾" strip fabric Cut **1** 4½" piece of ½" elastic	Cut **1** 5½" x 1¾" strip fabric Cut **1** 4" x 1¾" strip fabric
L-XL	Cut **2** 10½" x 1¼" *strips fabric* Cut **1 each** 5" x ½" hook-and-loop tape	Cut **1** 8" x 1¾" strip fabric Cut **1** 5" piece of ½" elastic	Cut **1** 6" x 1¾" strip fabric Cut **1** 4" x 1¾" strip fabric

TABLE: Back Strap Cutting Measurements

Assemble the Hat

1 Fuse the interfacing to the wrong sides of the cap front, cap side, cap back, and outer brim pieces according to the manufacturer's instructions.

2 Place a **cap side** piece against a corresponding **back** piece, right sides facing. Align the double-notched edges. Stitch ¼" from the aligned edges. Trim the seam allowance slightly, then press open. Finish the seams with single fold bias tape as described in the "Covering a Seam with Single Fold Bias Tape" sidebar on page 36. *Repeat with the other cap back and cap side pieces.*

Place a **cap front** piece against a corresponding side/back assembly. Align the single-notched edges. Stitch ¼" from the aligned edges. Trim, press, and finish the seams with single fold bias tape. (See Figure 2.) *Repeat with the other cap front and cap back/side pieces.*

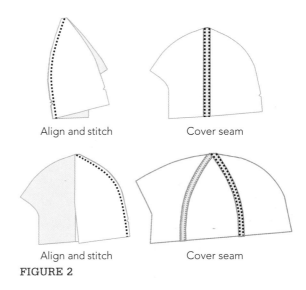

Align and stitch

Cover seam

Align and stitch

Cover seam

FIGURE 2

3 Place the 2 cap front/side/back assemblies together, right sides facing. Align the ends and center seams, then pin. Stitch together, ¼" from the aligned edges, leaving a ¼" opening in the center for button insertion. Make sure to backstitch at the beginning and end of the stitching. **NOTE:** *Omit the center opening if you are not adding a button.* Trim, press, and finish the seams with single fold bias tape. (See Figure 3.)

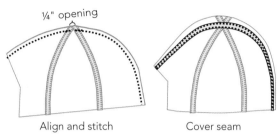

Align and stitch   Cover seam

FIGURE 3

4 The next step is to finish the cap back opening with single fold bias tape. Open out one edge of the bias tape. With the right sides facing, align the end and open edge of the tape with the back opening corner. Pin into place. Align and pin the tape into place along the length of the opening, then cut the tape flush with the end. Stitch ¼" from the aligned edges. Snip the seam allowance at the curves. Fold the tape over to the wrong side and press the tape to the shape of the opening. A tiny bit of the right side of the cap fabric should be visible at the edge. Edgestitch the tape into place (See Figure 4.)

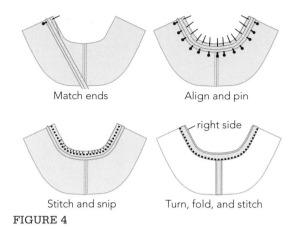

Match ends   Align and pin

Stitch and snip   Turn, fold, and stitch

FIGURE 4

5 Place the **outer brim** pieces together, right sides facing, and align the edges. Stitch ¼" from the un-notched front brim edge. Use your scissors to notch the seam allowance near the curves. Turn right side out. Work the edge between your fingers to fully roll out the seam, and press. Insert the **inner brim** piece (interfacing) so that the front edges are sitting on top of the seam allowance. Work the back edges up so that they are in line with the inner brim on both sides. Press to set. Topstitch ¼" from the front edge of the brim. **OPTIONAL:** Make additional lines of topstitching spaced ¼" apart. (See Figure 5.)

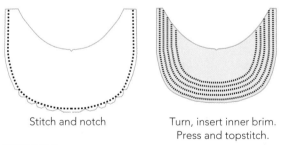

Stitch and notch   Turn, insert inner brim.
                              Press and topstitch.

FIGURE 5

6 For best results, attach the brim one side at a time. Lay the brim out with the top side facing up. Place front of the cap on the brim with the right sides facing. Match the center seam with the notch in the brim. Pin into place. Continue aligning and pinning in small sections until you reach one end of the brim. Stitch ⅜" from the aligned edges, taking care to avoid puckers in the cap fabric. Pin the other side of the brim as described for the first side. Due to the shape of the cap, you will be working inside of the dome. Carefully stitch this side's brim to the cap with a ⅜" seam allowance. (See Figure 6.)

Match centers   Align and pin one side

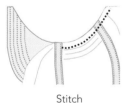

Stitch aligned side   Align, pin, and stitch other side

FIGURE 6

7 Make snips in the cap/brim seam allowance, taking care to not snip the stitching. Turn the cap wrong side out. Work the cap/brim seam allowance up towards the wrong side of the cap and press. Fold the adjacent bottom raw edges of the cap up ⅜" towards the wrong side and press. (See Figure 7.)

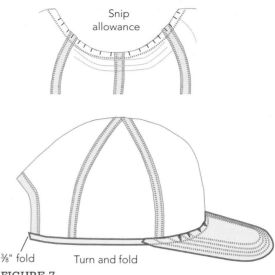

Snip allowance

⅜" fold   Turn and fold

FIGURE 7

8 Place the **cap band** pieces together, right sides facing. Stitch together, ¼" from the edges, leaving one short end open for turning. Trim the seam allowance at the corners. Turn the band right side out. Fully roll out the seams and press. Turn the unfinished edges under ¼" to the wrong side and press. Edgestitch into place. Fold the band in half widthwise and mark the center with a pin. (See Figure 8.)

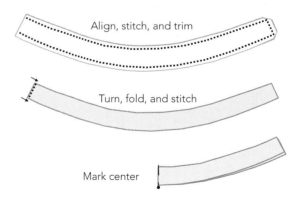

Align, stitch, and trim

Turn, fold, and stitch

Mark center

FIGURE 8

9 Apply a 2" or 3" length of basting tape to the seam allowance at the center of the brim and remove the backing. Place the long curved edge of the **band** just above the cap/brim stitching. The pin-marked center of the band should be in line with the center front seam of the cap. Use basting tape to adhere the band to the rest of the brim and folded bottom edges of the cap. The ends of the band should be in line with those of the cap. Pin the top of the band to the cap to keep it out of the way during the stitching process. Turn the cap so the right side is facing out. Make sure the band is not visible on the outside of the cap. Working on the right side of the cap, edgestitch the band into place from one end to the other. (See Figure 9.)

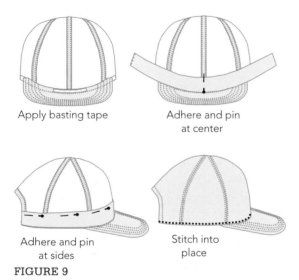

Apply basting tape

Adhere and pin at center

Adhere and pin at sides

Stitch into place

FIGURE 9

10 Construct and add the back strap fastener of your choice according to one of the instruction sets below:

a. Hook-and-loop Back Strap option. Fold the fastener strips in half widthwise, right sides facing in. Stitch ¼" from each of the long edges. Trim the seam allowance at the corners. Turn right side out and press. Use a glue stick to adhere the hook tape to one strap and the loop tape to the other piece. Sew the tape

pieces into place by edgestitching around the perimeter. Sandwich the hook tape piece between the band and the cap on the left-hand side. The hook side should be facing out, and the raw end of the fastener should be about ½" from the cap opening. Stitch into place through all layers. Repeat with the hook tape piece on the other side, but this time the loop tape side should be facing down. (See Figure 10a.)

Align, stitch, and trim

Turn, then glue on hook-and-loop tape, edgestitch into place

Insert and stitch hook tape strap

Insert and stitch loop tape strap

FIGURE 10a

b. Scrunched (Elastic) Back Strap option. Fold the fabric strip in half lengthwise, right side facing in. Stitch ¼" from the long edge. Turn right side out. Use a safety pin to insert the elastic into the fabric tube. Draw the elastic through until the end is flush with the opposite opening. Stitch the elastic into place ¼" from the end. Arrange the tube so the other end is flush with the elastic. Stitch into place ¼" from the end. Sandwich one end of the scrunched strap between the band and the cap with the raw edge, about ½" from the cap opening. Stitch into place through all layers, ¼" from the opening edge. Repeat insertion and stitching for the other end, making sure you do not introduce any twists. (See Figure 10b.)

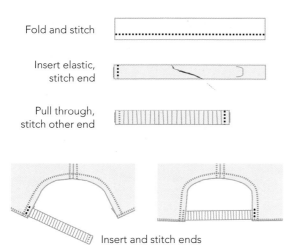

Fold and stitch

Insert elastic, stitch end

Pull through, stitch other end

Insert and stitch ends

FIGURE 10b

c. Buckle Back Strap option. Fold the longer fabric strip in half lengthwise, right side facing in. Stitch ¼" from one long edge and one of the short edges. Trim the seam allowance at the corners. Turn right side out and press. Sandwich the raw end of this fabric strap between the band and the cap on the left-hand side. The raw edge should be about ½" from the cap opening. Stitch into place through all layers. Fold the shorter fabric strap in half lengthwise, right side facing in. Stitch ¼" from the long edge. Turn right side out and press. Slip the fabric tube through the buckle center. Bring the short ends together so that the working parts of the buckle are on the outside. Turn the hat wrong side out and pull the band down and away from the cap on the left-hand side. Place the aligned ends of the buckle-holding strap atop the band. The raw edges should be about ½" from the opening, and the strap side should be flush with the cap seam. Stitch the strap into place against the band layers. Refold the band. Tack the top edge of the band into place near the opening, just above the top edge of the strap. (See Figure 10c.) This will leave a gap for inserting the end of the strap, if desired.

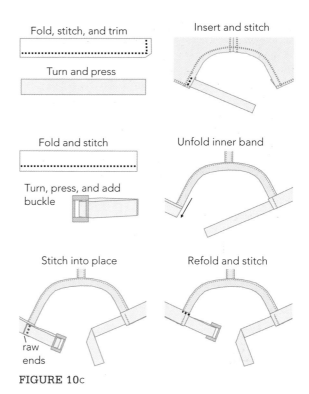

Fold, stitch, and trim

Turn and press

Insert and stitch

Fold and stitch

Turn, press, and add buckle

Unfold inner band

Stitch into place

raw ends

Refold and stitch

FIGURE 10c

11 Cover the button according to the manufacturer's instructions. Insert the shank into the opening in the top of the cap. If you can feel the shank through the bias tape on the underside, you may be able to stick a hand needle through and sew into place. Otherwise, make a small hole in the bias tape and pull the shank through, then sew it into place. (See Figure 11.)

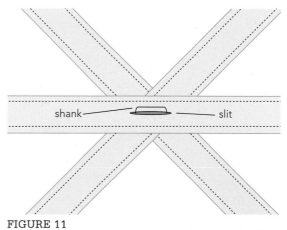

shank — slit

FIGURE 11

Do-Rag

DO-RAG

By Jaime Morrison Curtis and Jacinda Boneau (Prudent Baby)

This "can-do" cap is built for the hardest of workers: cooks, mechanics, nurses, bricklayers, and so on. But it is just as functional (and tough-looking) for leisure activities like hiking and biking. The simple, one-piece design goes on in a snap and keeps you cool and collected. A bit of elastic beneath the mock tie ensures a perfect fit. You can use a solid fabric for a no-nonsense approach, or have some serious fun with novelty prints.

Sizes: XS–L (Toddler–Adult)

Skill Level: Beginner/Intermediate

Materials

- ½ yard lightweight woven fabric. The designer used quilter's cotton for this project. Other possibilities include batiks or broadcloth.
- 3" length of ¼" wide elastic
- Safety pin to insert elastic
- OPTIONAL: Tailor's ham

Cut the Pattern Pieces

From the fabric: Cut 1 piece from the main cap pattern (on a fold). Cut 2 pieces each from the tail pattern and the tie pattern.

From the elastic: Cut a 2½" length.

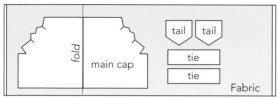

FIGURE 1: Cutting Layout

Assemble the Hat

1 Place the 2 **tail** pieces together, right sides facing and align the edges. Stitch together, ¼" from the un-notched side and bottom edges. Trim the seam allowance at the points. Turn right side out and press. **For *each* tie piece:** Fold the strip in half lengthwise, right side facing in. Stitch ¼" from the aligned long edge and 1 short edge. Trim the seam allowance at the points. Turn right side out and press. (See Figure 2.)

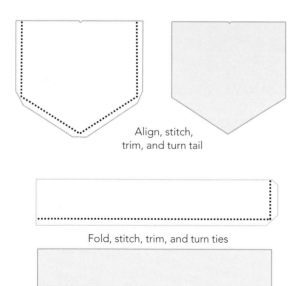

Align, stitch, trim, and turn tail

Fold, stitch, trim, and turn ties

FIGURE 2

2 Fold the front (longest) raw edge of the **main cap** piece over ¼" to the wrong side and press. Make a second ¼" fold to the wrong side and press. Stitch the fold into place, ⅛" from the folded edge. Place the tail on the back edge of the main cap piece and align the notches. The right side (the one that will be on the outside of the finished cap) of the tail should be facing the right side of the main cap fabric. Stitch ⅝" from the aligned edges. (See Figure 3.)

Fold and stitch

Align and stitch

FIGURE 3

3 Edge finish the length of the back edge with a serger or with zigzag stitching. Pull the tail up and away from the main cap. Press the seam allowance down against the wrong side of the main cap. Fold the back edge over ¼" at the ends. Press each side so the fold neatly transitions from ¼" at the end to ⅝" at the tail. (See Figure 4.)

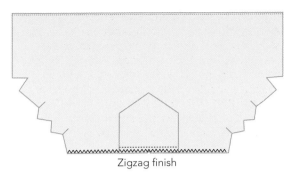

Zigzag finish

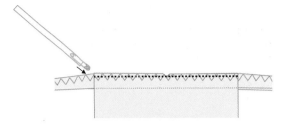

Stitch casing, insert elastic

Stitch end into place

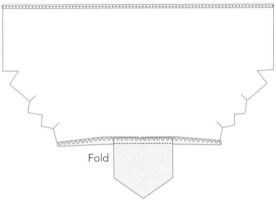

Fold

FIGURE 4

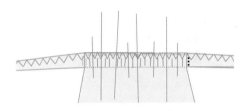

Pull through and stitch other end

FIGURE 5

4 Stitch ⅛" from the top edge of the tail to form a casing. Use a safety pin to insert the elastic behind the folded edge. Draw the elastic through until the end of the elastic is about ½" from the side of the tail. Stitch into place by sewing back and forth just beside the tail. Pull the elastic through and remove the safety pin. Adjust the elastic so that the end of the elastic is about ½" beyond the other side of the tail. Stitch into place just beside the tail. (See Figure 5.)

5 Lay the cap piece out with the right side facing up. Pick up one corner, and fold the fabric over so that the top two points (labeled a and b) are together, and the short edges are in line. Press. Stitch ¾" from the short edge, all the way up to the crease. (See Figure 6.)

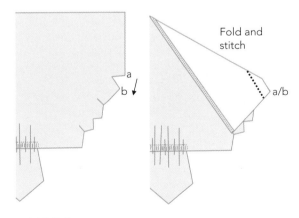

Fold and stitch

a

b

a/b

FIGURE 6

6 Flip the fabric over so the wrong side is facing up. Press the ¾" seam allowance down in the direction of the back edge. *Repeat* the folding and stitching process from step 5 and the pressing process from this step on the *other* side of the main cap (with right side facing up again). Then fold the **side** edges over 1" (with wrong side facing). (See Figure 7.) Repeat on the other side edge (with wrong side facing).

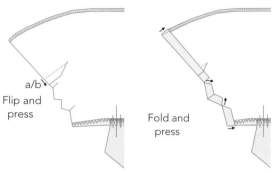

FIGURE 7

7 Fold the top edge over 2" to the wrong side and press. Edgestitch ⅛" from the *fold*. (See Figure 8.)

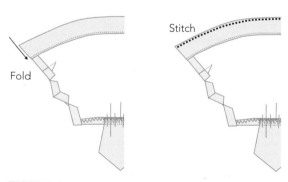

FIGURE 8

8 Flip up the front fold you just made. On one side, place a tie just below the seam with the raw end 1" from the side's folded edge. Stitch into place, ½" from the end. Repeat to attach the second tie on the other side. Refold the front fold. (See Figure 9.)

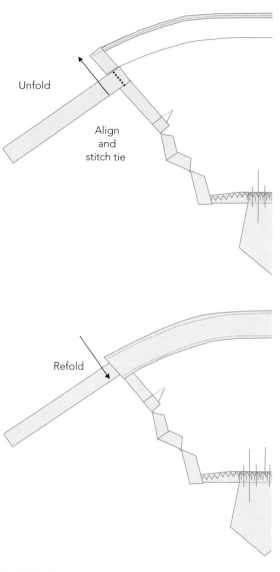

FIGURE 9

9 Lay out the cap piece with the right side facing up. Fold the top edge over 2" to the right side. This new fold should be in line with the original double-folded front edge. Stitch into place, ⅛" from the aligned side edges. (See Figure 10.) Repeat on the other side.

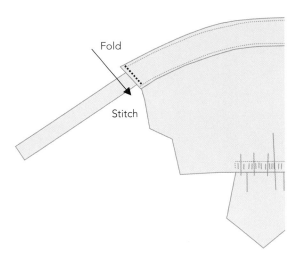

Fold

Stitch

FIGURE 10

10 Lay the cap piece out with the wrong side facing up. With the wrong side facing in, bring the middle point (labeled c) over to meet the bottom point (labeled d). Stitch ⅛" from the aligned folded edges. (See Figure 11.) Repeat on the other side.

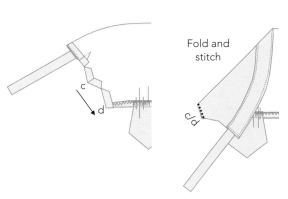

Fold and stitch

c

d

c/d

FIGURE 11

11 Arrange the cap so the back right side is facing up. Fold the stitched edge from the previous step over so that it is about ¼" from the casing and perpendicular to the bottom edge. Stitch into place, right over the existing stitching. Repeat on the other side. Swing the side front edge over so that it is right next to the casing and perpendicular to the bottom edge. Stitch into place, right over the existing stitching. Stitch the layers into place at the bottom edge from the side of the tail to the first adjacent fold. (See Figure 12.) Repeat on the other side. Tie the ties into a knot.

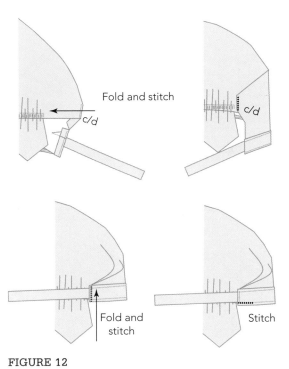

Fold and stitch
c/d

c/d

Fold and stitch

Stitch

FIGURE 12

12 **OPTIONAL:** Place the do-rag on the recipient's head. Arrange the back folds, tucking them in to give a more rounded shape. Place on a tailor's ham (see chapter 1) and press to set.

EXTRA-EXTRA NEWSKID CAP

By Karen LePage (One Girl Circus)

Read all about it! Your little cutie will surely make headlines in this newsy-style cap. The design features a fitted band; a full, six-pieced crown; and a stand-out brim. It is completely reversible, so you can show off two favorite fabrics. Use traditional black and white for an old-time look, or go full color for trendy, fashion-forward flair.

Sizes: XXS–S (Baby–Youth)

Skill Level: Beginner/Intermediate

Materials

- 2 pieces (⅜ yard each) of light- to mediumweight woven fashion fabric. The designer used quilter's cottons and baby wale corduroy for this project. Other possibilities include broadcloth, canvas, denim, or suitings.
- ⅛ yard woven cotton fusible interfacing (see chapter 1) for the brim

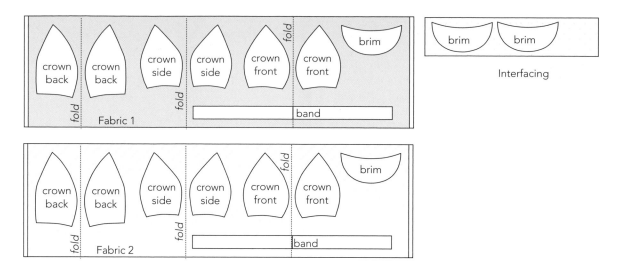

FIGURE 1: Cutting Layout

Cut the Pattern Pieces

From fabric 1: Cut 2 mirror-image pieces *each* from the crown front, crown side, and crown back patterns (near folds). Cut 1 piece from the band pattern (on a fold). Cut 1 piece from the brim pattern.

From fabric 2: Cut 2 mirror-image pieces *each* from the crown front, crown side, and crown back patterns (near folds). Cut 1 piece from the band pattern (on a fold). Cut 1 piece from the brim pattern.

From the fusible interfacing: Cut 2 pieces from the brim pattern.

Assemble the Hat

1 Fuse the interfacing to the wrong sides of both brim pieces according to the manufacturer's instructions.

2 Place the **fabric brim** pieces together, right sides facing, and align the edges. Stitch ¼" from the front brim edge. Make notches in the seam allowance near the curves. Turn right side out. Work the edge between your fingers to fully roll out the seam and press. Topstitch ¼" from the front edge of the brim. (See Figure 2.)

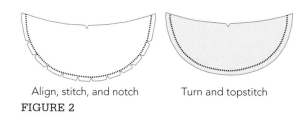

Align, stitch, and notch   Turn and topstitch

FIGURE 2

3 **For each *band* piece:** Fold in half widthwise, right side facing in. Stitch ¼" from the aligned short edges. Press the seam allowance open. With the fabric 2 side of the brim facing the right side of the fabric 2 band, match the notch in the brim with the notch in the band. Align and pin the flanking edges. Stitch together, ⅛" from the aligned edges. (See Figure 3.)

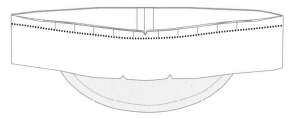

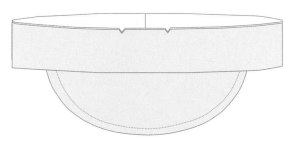

Align, stitch, and snip

Fold and stitch (x2)

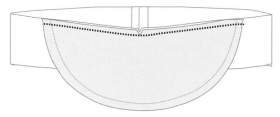

Align and stitch

FIGURE 3

4 With the right sides facing, slip the fabric 1 *band* over the fabric 2 *band* and align the single-notched edges. *Make sure the brim is sandwiched between the two band pieces.* Stitch ¼" from the aligned edges. Snip the seam allowance at the curved inner brim edges. Fold the band pieces back and away from the brim so the wrong sides are facing. Align the edges, matching the two notches. Work the bottom edge between your fingers to fully roll out the seam and press. (See Figure 4.) Set the band/brim assembly aside.

Fold and press

FIGURE 4

5 With the right sides facing, align the double-notched edge of one of the fabric 1 **crown side** pieces with one of the corresponding fabric 1 **crown back** pieces. Pin, stretching the fabric as needed to match the notches and points. Stitch together, ¼" from the aligned edges. Press the seam allowances open. Repeat with the remaining fabric 1 crown side and crown back pieces. ***For each pair:*** Align the single-notched edge of the **crown side** piece to the corresponding **crown front** piece, right sides facing. Pin, then stitch ¼" from the aligned edges. Place the two fabric 1 hat halves together, right sides facing. Align the front and back edges, matching the notches, centers, and corners. Stitch together ¼" from the aligned edges. (See Figure 5.) Press the seam allowances open. Turn the crown dome right side out.

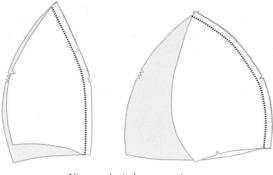

Align and stitch crown pieces

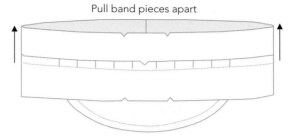

Pull band pieces apart

FIGURE 5

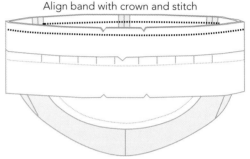

Align band with crown and stitch

FIGURE 6

6 Repeat step 7 with the fabric 2 crown pieces.

7 Flip the band assembly so the fabric 2 side is facing out. Pull the fabric 2 band down and away from the fabric 1 band so that it is against the fabric 2 side of the brim. With the right (fabric 1) sides facing, slip the band over the crown. Match the front notches and the back seams, then align the edges in between. Stitch ¼" from the aligned edges. (See Figure 6.)

8 Pull the fabric 1 crown away from the band, then press the seam allowance down against the crown. Tuck the brim down against the fabric 1 crown, then insert the fabric 2 crown into the fabric 2 band, right sides facing. Match the front notches and the back seams, then align the edges in between. Stitch ¼" from the aligned edges, leaving a 3" opening at the center back. (See Figure 7.)

Turn crown/bands inside out,
insert other crown

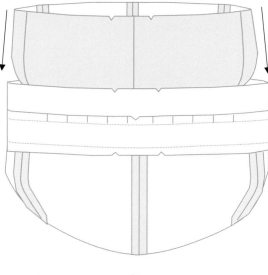

Stitch   3"

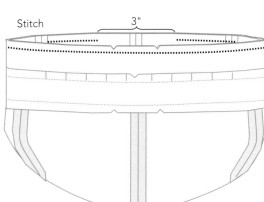

FIGURE 7

9 Turn the hat right side out through the opening. Arrange the fabric crown/band seam allowance so it is down against the crown. The fold at the opening should be flush with the rest of the seam. Pin the layers of the crown together near the band seam. Topstitch into place along the crown, ⅛" from the crown band seam. Work the bottom edge of the band between your fingers to fully roll out the seam. Press, then topstitch ⅛" from the bottom edge. (See Figure 8.)

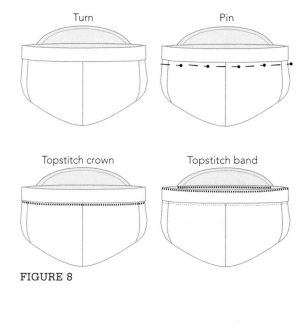

Turn   Pin

Topstitch crown   Topstitch band

FIGURE 8

Eddie Cap

EDDIE CAP

By Irene Rodegerdts (Mushroom Villagers)

This stylish cap works for guys and gals alike. Based on the traditional train engineer's cap, this design features a sturdy brim and a pleated crown. You can construct it from work-weight canvases or denim to get a classically casual style, or go with wool plaids or houndstooth checks for a dressier, prepster look.

Sizes: S–L (Youth–Adult)

Skill Level: Beginner/Intermediate

Materials

- ⅝ yard medium- to heavyweight woven fashion fabric. The designer used wool for this project. Other possibilities include canvas, corduroy, or denim.
- ⅛ yard lightweight fusible interfacing (see chapter 1) for the brim
- OPTIONAL: Fusible webbing (see chapter 1) for the band. To cut the needed length in a continuous strip, purchase 1 roll or ¾ yard.
- OPTIONAL EMBELLISHMENTS: See the appendix for embellishment options and instructions.

Cut the Pattern Pieces

From the fashion fabric: Cut 1 piece from the crown pattern (on a fold). Cut 2 pieces from the brim pattern. Cut 1 strip each from the inner and outer band patterns (on folds). *NOTE: The strips are cut on the bias, so make the folds at a 45-degree angle relative to the selvage edge.*

From the fusible interfacing: Cut 1 piece using the brim pattern.

From the fusible webbing: Cut 1 piece using the outer band pattern (on a fold). (This optional component holds the fold in place during the final attachment step.)

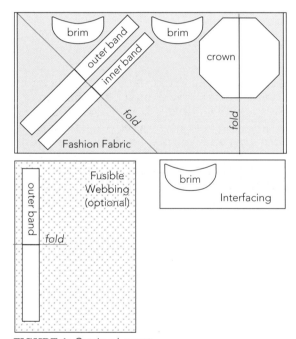

FIGURE 1: Cutting Layout

Assemble the Hat

1 Fuse the interfacing to the wrong side of 1 of the brim pieces (preferably the one that will be on the top side in the finished cap) according to the manufacturer's instructions. **OPTIONAL:** Fuse the webbing to the wrong side of the outer band according to the manufacturer's instructions.

2 Place the **brim** pieces together, right sides facing, and align the edges. Stitch ¼" from the un-notched front brim edge. Snip notches in the seam allowance near the curves. Turn right side out. Work the edge between your fingers to fully roll out the seam and press. Topstitch ¼" from the front edge of the brim. **OPTIONAL:** Make 2 to 3 additional lines of topstitching spaced ¼" apart. (See Figure 2.)

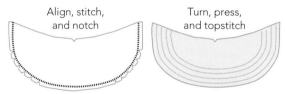

Align, stitch, and notch   Turn, press, and topstitch

FIGURE 2

3 Zigzag or serger finish the un-notched long edge of the *inner* (narrower) band. **For each band piece:** Fold in half widthwise, right side facing in. Stitch ½" from the aligned short edges. (See Figure 3.) Press the seam allowance open. *NOTE: If you have added fusible webbing to the outer band, make sure you do **not** touch the exposed webbing with the iron because it will melt the fusible webbing.*

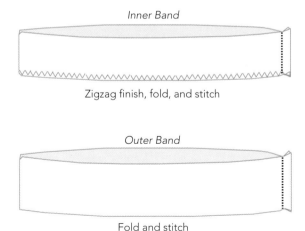

Inner Band

Zigzag finish, fold, and stitch

Outer Band

Fold and stitch

FIGURE 3

4 With the right sides facing, match the notch in the **brim** with the notch in the **outer band.** Align and pin the flanking edges. Stitch together, ⅜" from the aligned edges. With the right sides facing, slip the inner band over the outer band and align the notched edges. Make sure the brim is sandwiched between the 2 band pieces. Stitch ½" from the aligned edges. Snip the seam allowance at the curved inner brim edges. (See Figure 4.)

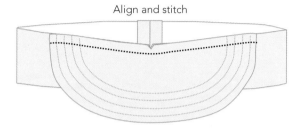

Align and stitch

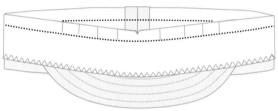

Put bands together,
align, stitch, and snip

FIGURE 4

5 Separate the band layers, and arrange them so the brim is pointed down and against the outer band, and the seam allowance is pointed up and against the inner band. Fold the raw edge of the outer band over ½" to the wrong side. Press to set. (See Figure 5.)

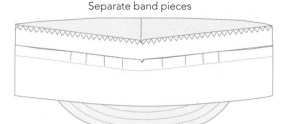

Separate band pieces

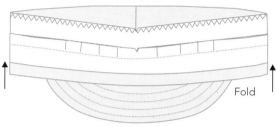

Fold

FIGURE 5

6 The next step is to create 8 pleats in the crown. Lay the crown piece out with the right side facing up. **For each pleat:** Bring 2 adjacent sides together, right sides facing, to make a diagonal fold at the corner. Place a pin 1" from the point, perpendicular to the aligned edges. Pull the layers apart, and arrange the pleat so it is pointing toward the notch and flush with the edges. Pin the pleat into place, then remove the first pin. *NOTE: After the first few pleats, you may become comfortable enough with the pleating process to eliminate the first pinning step.* After pleating all 8 points, the crown should have a bowl shape. Each pleat should be straight, and the raw edges should be even with one another (See Figure 6.)

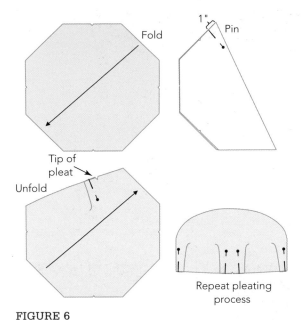

FIGURE 6

7 Stitch ¼" from the bottom edge of the cap to set 3 pairs of pleats. *Leave the pair of pleats that will be in the back unstitched (but still pinned) at this point so that minor adjustments can be made.* (See Figure 7.)

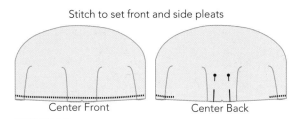

FIGURE 7

8 With the wrong sides facing, place the crown on top of the inner band so that the bottom edge of the crown is touching the edge of the band/brim seam allowance. The front center notch of the crown should be in line with that of the brim and outer band. Pin into place. Align and pin the sides, working towards the back seam. Match the back notch of the crown with the center seam. If needed, symmetrically adjust the pleats at the back edge. Use a long, loose basting stitch to attach the crown to the inner band, about ½" from the bottom edge of the crown. (See Figure 8.)

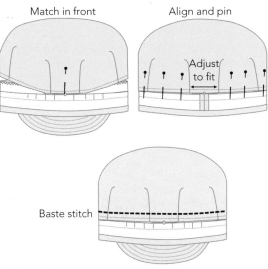

FIGURE 8

9 Flip the outer band up so the wrong side is against the right side of the crown. Pin the layers together. Topstitch into place along the band, ⅛" from the top edge. Use a walking foot if you have one; otherwise, take your time and make sure the layers do not shift. (See Figure 9.) Remove the basting stitches.

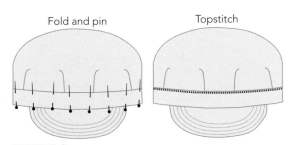

FIGURE 9

10 **OPTIONAL:** Sew on any embellishments you want. (Refer to the appendix for directions on making different embellishment options.)

Little Engineer Cap

LITTLE ENGINEER CAP

By Anneliese S. (Aesthetic Nest)

Toot, toot . . . all aboard the cuteness train! This cap is designed for the tiniest of engineers. Use classic blue-and-white stripes to make the perfect accessory for a visit with your tot's favorite engine, or for playtime around the train table. This adorable style looks great in other fun fabrics as well. For a feminine touch, you can add a sweet bow to the back. A bit of elastic inside the band makes for a comfortable-fitting cap that stays put, even when the wearer is constantly in motion.

Sizes: NB–XS (Newborn–Toddler)

Skill Level: Beginner/Intermediate

Materials

- **Fashion fabric:** ½ yard light- to mediumweight woven fashion fabric. The designer used a patchwork madras for this project. Other possibilities include canvas, corduroy, denim, homespun, or quilter's cottons.
- **Lining fabric:** ⅜ yard lightweight woven fabric. The designer used muslin for this project. Other possibilities include broadcloth or quilter's cotton.
- ¾ yard mediumweight fusible interfacing (see chapter 1) for the brim and band
- 3" length of 1"-wide elastic
- Safety pin to insert elastic
- OPTIONAL: ⅛ yard light- to mediumweight contrasting fabric for bow

Cut the Pattern Pieces

From the fashion fabric: Cut 1 piece from the crown pattern. Cut 2 pieces from the brim pattern. Cut 2 pieces from the band pattern (on folds).

From the lining fabric: Cut 1 piece from the crown pattern.

From the fusible interfacing: Cut 2 pieces from the brim pattern. Cut 2 pieces from the band pattern (on folds).

From the elastic: Cut a 3" length.

Assemble the Hat

1 Fuse interfacing to the wrong sides of the band and brim pieces according to the manufacturer's instructions.

2 Place the crown pieces together, wrong sides facing, and match the notches. Stitch together, ⅜" from the aligned edges. Lay out the crown circle with the fashion fabric side up and the double notch at the top. **For each pleat:** Bring a pair of notches together in the direction indicated on the pattern. Arrange the resulting pleat so that it is in line with the edge, and pin into place. After making all of the pleats, stitch all but the back pair into place, ⅜" from the edge. (See Figure 2.)

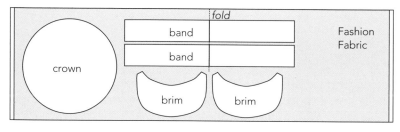

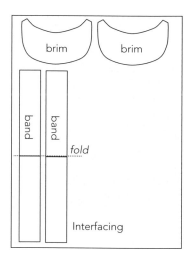

FIGURE 1: Cutting Layout

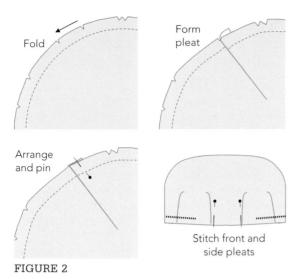

Fold

Form pleat

Arrange and pin

Stitch front and side pleats

FIGURE 2

3 **For each band piece:** Fold in half widthwise, right side facing in. Stitch ½" from the aligned short edges. Press the seam allowance open. **For the _inner_ band only:** Fold the double-notched long edge over ½" towards the wrong side. (See Figure 3.)

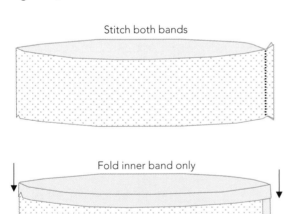

Stitch both bands

Fold inner band only

FIGURE 3

4 With the right sides of the fashion fabric facing, slip the **outer (non-folded) band** over the **crown** and align the double notches. Pin into

place. Align and pin the adjacent crown and band edges, working towards the back. Center the back seam between the two back pleats. If needed, remove the pins and adjust the two back pleats so that the crown fits into the band. Stitch together, ½" from the aligned edges. Pull the band away from the crown, and press the seam allowance down against the band. (See Figure 4.)

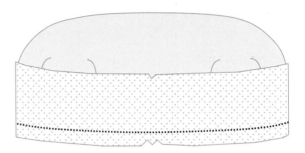

Align and stitch

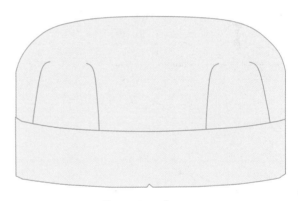

Separate and press

FIGURE 4

5 Place the brim pieces together, right sides facing. Stitch the layers together, ½" from the outer (un-notched) edges. Trim the seam allowance down to ⅛". Turn the brim right side out and work the edge between your fingers to fully roll out the seam and press. Stitch the layers together, ⅜" from the aligned _inner_ edges. Topstitch ⅛" from the outer edges. (See Figure 5.)

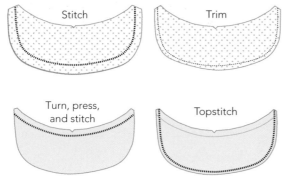

FIGURE 5

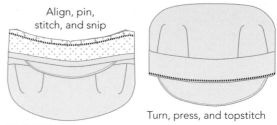

FIGURE 7

6 Place the right side (the one that will be on top in the finished cap) of the **brim** against the right side of the **outer band** and match the notches. Align and pin the edges. Stitch the brim to the outer band, ⅜" from the aligned edges. (See Figure 6.)

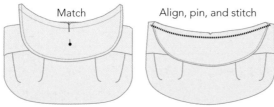

FIGURE 6

7 Slip the inner band over the outer band, right sides facing, and align the single-notched edges and pin. The brim should be sandwiched between the two band layers. Stitch together, ½" from the aligned edges. Snip the seam allowance at the curved inner brim edge. Flip the inner band over to the inside of the hat. Work the bottom edge of the hat between your fingers to fully roll out the seam and press. Topstitch ⅛" from the edge. (See Figure 7.)

8 Stitch along the band from one back pleat to the other, ⅛" from the top folded edge. *Make sure the stitching catches the folded edge of the inner band inside.* Use a safety pin to insert the elastic into the casing formed by the stitching, between the 2 band layers. Pull the elastic through until the end of it is ½" from the position of the pleat. Stitch into place, ½" from the elastic end (just below the pleat). Arrange the other end of the elastic so that it is ½" beyond the second pleat. Stitch into place, ½" from the end. (See Figure 8.)

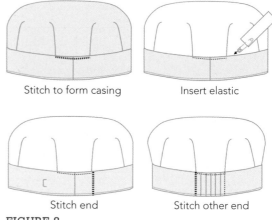

FIGURE 8

9 Arrange the folded edge of the inner band so that it covers the stitching joining the crown to the outer band. For best results, hand baste or use basting tape to set into place. Working on the outside of the hat, stitch along the band, ⅛" from the seam. Make sure the stitching catches the folded edge of the inner band. (See Figure 9.)

10 **OPTIONAL:** Construct a bow as described in the appendix. Hand sew the bow into place over the casing in the back of the cap.

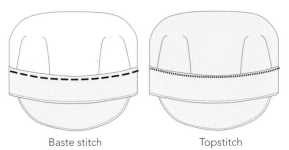

Baste stitch   Topstitch

FIGURE 9

7

HAVING FUN

Andrea/Andrew
Hat

ANDREA/ANDREW HAT

By Linda and Scott Hansen (Miss Mabel Studio and Blue Nickel Studios)

This fun, versatile hat looks good on girls and guys alike! Go wild with fabric combos—you can mix and match a few favorite prints or make every single piece unique. The basic hat has a straight brim that is perfect for adornment with trims and embellishments. The elongated hat is worn toque-style, with the brim flipped up. The pointed hat has a whimsical, jester-like quality . . . bring on the bells and whistles! All styles are reversible, so you get two hats in one!

Sizes: S–L (Youth–Adult)

Skill Level: Beginner/Intermediate

Materials

- **Fabric:** You can make the hat with solid fabric or alternating combinations on each side. Choose 1–6 light- to mediumweight fabrics for each side (2–12 fabrics total). Possibilities include broadcloth, homespuns, linen, or quilter's cottons.
  - **Basic or pointed hat:** You will need 1 fat quarter (18" × 22") or ⅜ yard (off the bolt) of each fabric.
  - **Solid elongated hat:** You will need ⅝ yard of each print so you can orient the pieces side-by-side and parallel to the selvage edge.
  - **For an elongated hat with alternating prints:** Each fat quarter or ¼ linear yard yields 2 pieces when oriented perpendicular to the selvage edge. Purchase enough fabric to cut 12 pieces in the desired combination.
- OPTIONAL EMBELLISHMENTS: Possibilities include trims like ball fringe and rickrack (¾ yard each), fabric yo-yos (made from scraps—see the appendix), buttons, bells, or beads.

Cut the Pattern Pieces

Cut 12 wedge pieces (6 for each side of the hat) from the desired combination of fabrics.

Basic and Pointed Options

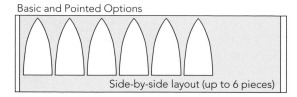

Side-by-side layout (up to 6 pieces)

Elongated Option

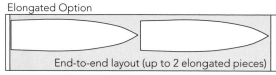

End-to-end layout (up to 2 elongated pieces)

FIGURE 1: Cutting Layout

Assemble the Hat

1 This hat is pieced together in units of 3 (2 units for each side). Place the first 2 pieces together, right sides facing, and pin along one long edge. Stitch together, ¼" from the aligned edges. Press the seam allowance open. Place the third piece atop the existing pair, and align and pin one long edge. Stitch and press as described for the first pair. Set this assembly aside, and construct the next unit of 3. Repeat until you have 4 units total. (See Figure 2.)

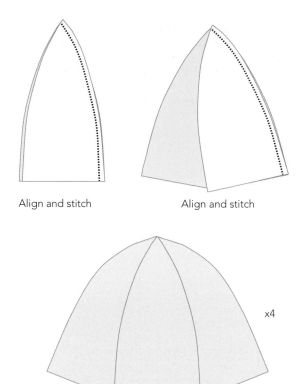

Align and stitch

Align and stitch

x4

FIGURE 2

2 Put 2 units together, right sides facing, and align one side. Pin together, making sure the seams match. Stitch from the bottom edge up to the center seam. Repeat on the other side. Align and stitch the remaining 2 units as described. (See Figure 3.)

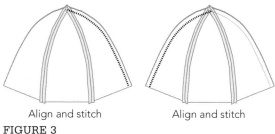

Align and stitch

Align and stitch

FIGURE 3

3 Place the completed crowns together, right sides facing. Align the bottom edges. **For the basic and pointed options:** Match the seams. **For the elongated option:** Either match the seams as shown in the figure, or offset them for a staggered look when the base is flipped up. (See Figure 4.)

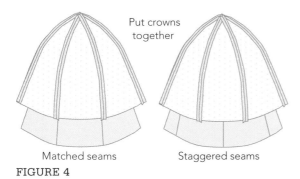

Put crowns together

Matched seams   Staggered seams

FIGURE 4

4 Stitch ¼" from the aligned edges, leaving one section open for turning. Turn the hat right side out through the opening. Tuck one section of the hat into the other. Work the bottom edge between your fingers to fully roll out the seam. Arrange the edges at the opening so the folds are flush with the rest of the edge. Press, then topstitch around the base of the hat, ⅛" from the edge. (See Figure 5.)

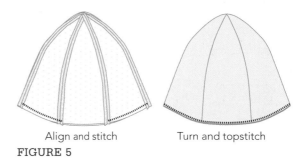

Align and stitch   Turn and topstitch

FIGURE 5

5 Embellish as desired. (See the appendix for instructions on how to make fabric yo-yos, as suggested in the Materials list.)

Coonskin Hat

COONSKIN HAT

By Betz White (betzwhite.com)

This charming hat harkens back to the 1950s, when every boy wanted to be Davy Crockett. This modern adaptation is fun and easy to make for your favorite frontiersman. It features a lined crown and a striped "coon" tail. Made from faux fur, this hat is soft, warm, and critter-friendly.

Sizes: S–L (Child–Adult)

Skill Level: Beginner

Materials

- ¼ yard gray faux fur
- ¼ yard tan faux fur
- ¼ yard flannel or other soft, light- to mediumweight woven fabric for the lining
- A handful of polyester stuffing

Cut the Pattern Pieces

From the gray fur: Cut 1 piece using the crown pattern. Cut 2 pieces using the band pattern. Cut a 1½" × 18" strip.

From the tan fur: Cut 2 pieces using the tail pattern. Cut a 1½" × 18" strip.

From the lining fabric: Cut 1 piece using the crown pattern. Cut 2 pieces using the band pattern.

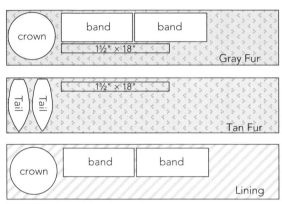

FIGURE 1: Cutting Layout

Assemble the Hat

1 Place the 2 **fur** band pieces together, right sides facing. Sew both sets of short ends together with a ¼" seam allowance. With the right sides facing, align the top edge of the fur band with the edge of the fur crown. Make sure the nap of the fur is pointing down in the finished hat. Match the crown's notches with the band's seams and pin together. Align and pin the edges in between. Stitch ¼" from the aligned edges. (See Figure 2.) Repeat the process with the **lining** pieces.

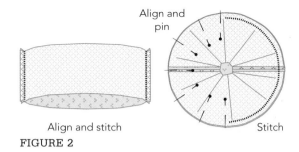

Align and stitch   Stitch

FIGURE 2

2 Place the fur hat inside the lining, right sides facing and side seams matching. Pin around the perimeter, then stitch with a ¼" seam allowance, leaving a 4" opening at the center back (halfway between the side seams). Turn right side out through the opening. Arrange the seam so a bit of the fur shows on the lining side. Edgestitch into place, ⅛" from the seam, except at the position of the opening. (See Figure 3.) **NOTE:** You can use the tip of a pin to pick out the fur from the seam and the stitching.

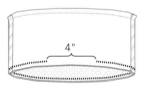

Put lining and hat together, stitch   Turn and edgestitch

FIGURE 3

3 Place the tail pieces together, right sides facing. Stitch together with a ¼" seam allowance, leaving the top straight edge open. Turn the tail right side out through the opening and stuff lightly with polyester stuffing. Cut fringe along one long side of *each* of the fur strips by snipping every ¼" with the tip of fabric shears, stopping ¼" from the opposite edge. *Make sure to cut the edge with overhanging fur so the nap points down in the finished hat.* **NOTE:** You can trim this edge with pinking shears before snipping, if desired, for a more natural "fuzzy tail" look. (See Figure 4.)

Stitch, turn,
and stuff

Snip

FIGURE 4

4 Lay the first gray strip across the tail with the fringe hanging down towards the tip. The top (un-snipped) edge of the strip should be about 1" from the tip of the tail. With hand needle and thread, sew the straight edge of the strip to the tail with a running stitch. Cut the strip where the ends meet on the underside and stitch the ends together at the top ¼". Repeat with the tan strip, overlapping the first strip by ½" to ¾". Continue applying strips in this fashion, alternating colors and ending ½" below the top of the tail. (See Figure 5.)

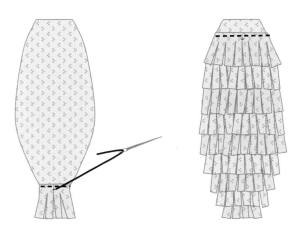

Hand stitch strips around tail

FIGURE 5

5 Fold and pin the seam allowances at the opening so they are flush with the bottom edge of the hat. Insert the top of the tail about ½" into the opening and baste stitch into place. Continue the edgestitching to close the opening and secure the tail. (See Figure 6.)

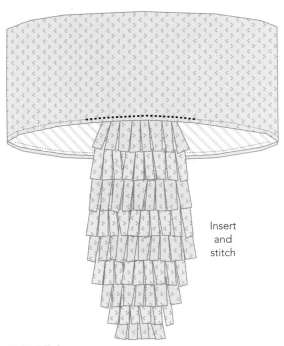

Insert and stitch

FIGURE 6

Crazy Patch
Bucket Hat

CRAZY PATCH BUCKET HAT

By Kim Christopherson (YouCanMakeThis.com)

Inspired by crazy quilts of the Victorian era, this hat is as fun to make as it is to wear. The close-fitting style has a vintage, yet thoroughly modern look. This hat is a great way to use those gorgeous scraps you can't bear to part with. Make a soft, lightweight hat from cotton prints, or you can go more decadent with fabrics like silk and velveteen. The whimsical patches are fantastic for showcasing small embroidery designs. Add buttons, trims, and ribbon roses for a true, over-the-top crazy quilt look.

Sizes: S–L (Youth–Adult)

Skill Level: Beginner/Intermediate

Materials

- ½ yard lightweight white muslin
- Assorted scraps of light- to mediumweight woven fabrics (forty to fifty 3–6" pieces). The designer used cottons, velveteens, and silks for this project. Other possibilities include corduroy, felt, satin, or wool.
- ⅝ yard lightweight woven fabric for the lining
- 1 yard heavyweight fusible interfacing (see chapter 1)
- Fabric marker
- Glue stick
- OPTIONAL TRIMS AND EMBELLISHMENTS: Possibilities include ribbons, lace, rickrack, ribbon roses, buttons, and embroideries (see the appendix for embellishment options and instructions)

Cut the Pattern Pieces

From the muslin: Cut six 6" × 11" rectangles and one 9" × 9" square.

From the lining fabric: Cut 1 piece each from the crown, band (on fold), and brim patterns (on fold).

From the interfacing: Cut 1 piece each from the crown, band (on fold), and brim patterns (on fold).

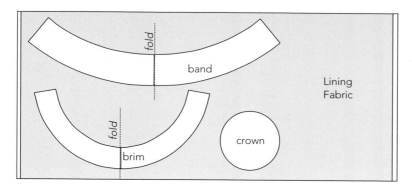

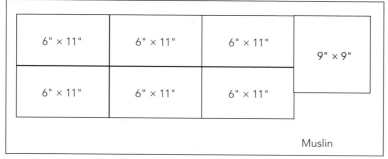

FIGURE 1: Cutting Layout

Trace the Patches

For each foundation section: Place a piece of muslin (rectangles for the 3 band and 3 brim pieces, the square for the crown piece) over the pattern sheet. Use your fabric marker to trace all of the lines and transfer the numbers onto the muslin. Make sure you use the appropriate outer line for the desired size.

Assemble the Hat

1 Fuse the interfacing to the wrong sides of the lining band, crown, and brim pieces according to the manufacturer's instructions.

2 **For *each* muslin foundation section:** Apply the glue stick to the inner perimeter of patch 1. Place the desired scrap on top of the section, right side facing up, and let set (a hot iron can greatly speed up this process). Fold the fabric back at each edge, and trim to match the lines. (See Figure 2.) Don't worry about making it perfect . . . in a crazy patch hat, anything goes! If you want to add a trim like rickrack or lace to this patch, now is the time to sew it into place so that the overhanging ends are worked into the seams.

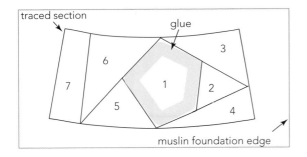

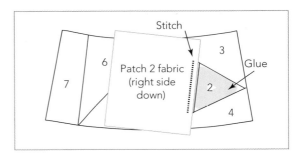

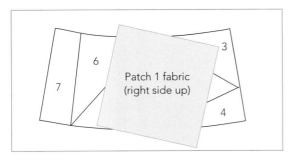

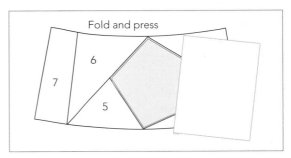

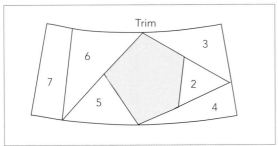

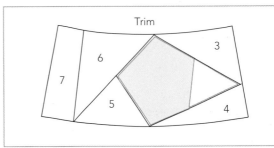

FIGURE 2

FIGURE 3

3 *Subsequent patches don't have to be cut to a specific shape before sewing, just make sure that they are larger than the area they need to cover, and have at least one straight edge.* Place the patch 2 scrap on top of patch 1, right sides facing, and align the edges at the patch 2 border. Stitch ¼" from the aligned edges, making sure to stop and start at the adjacent patch lines. Apply the glue stick to the inner perimeter of patch 2. Fold the scrap over to cover patch 2 and press the seam. After the glue has set, fold the fabric back and trim at the patch 2 edges. (See Figure 3.)

4 Repeat the alignment, stitching, pressing, gluing, and trimming process for the remainder of the patches, embellishing as desired. After all the patches are added to a foundation section, trim the muslin around the outer traced edges. (See Figure 4.) Repeat with the other foundation pieces. You should end up with 1 crown, 3 brim, and 3 band pieces.

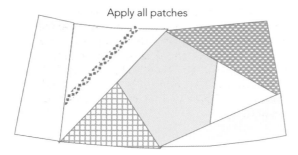

Apply all patches

Trim muslin foundation

FIGURE 4

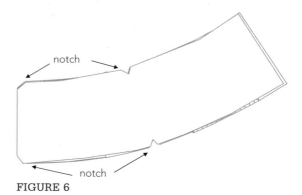

notch

notch

FIGURE 6

5 Place 2 of the patched **band** pieces together, right (patchwork) sides facing. Stitch together, ¼" from one of the short edges. Press the seam open. Repeat to add the remaining band foundation piece. (See Figure 5.) Sew the patched **brim** pieces together as described for the band pieces.

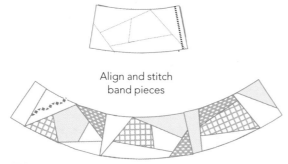

Align and stitch
band pieces

FIGURE 5

6 Fold the patched band and brim pieces in half and use the lining patterns as guides for cutting notches. (See Figure 6.) Make notches in the patched crown piece using the lining crown pattern as a guide.

7 Fold the **lining band** in half widthwise, right side facing in. Stitch ¼" from the aligned short edges. Press the seam allowance open. With the right sides facing, match the notches and seam of the top (smaller) edge of the lining band with the notches of the lining crown and pin. Align and pin the edges in between. Stitch the crown to the band, ¼" from the aligned edges. Trim the seam allowance to ⅛". Turn the band/crown assembly right side out. (See Figure 7.)

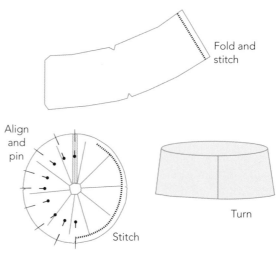

Fold and
stitch

Align
and
pin

Stitch

Turn

FIGURE 7

8 Fold the **lining brim** in half widthwise, right side facing in. Stitch ¼" from the aligned short edges. Press the seam allowance open. Slip the brim over the band so that the right sides are facing and the inner raw edges are in line with those of the band. Match the brim seams with the band seams and pin into place. Match other notches, and align and pin the edges in between. Stitch ¼" from the aligned edges, leaving a 2" opening in the back for turning. Flip the brim down and press the seam allowance up against the band. (See Figure 8.)

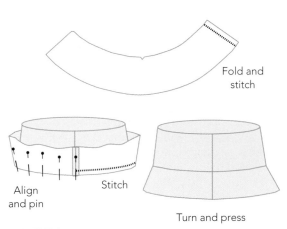

Fold and stitch

Align and pin

Stitch

Turn and press

FIGURE 8

9 Repeat steps 7–8 for the outer **patchwork** pieces. *On the last step, do not leave an opening, just stitch all the way around the aligned brim and band.* **NOTE:** If you are planning to add ribbon roses, buttons, or hand embroidery, now is a good time to do it.

10 Turn the lining pieces so the wrong sides are facing out. Place the lining over the patched outer hat, right sides facing. Align the outer brim edges, and arrange the lining seam so it is in the center back relative to the outer hat. Stitch the layers together, ¼" from the aligned edges. (See Figure 9.) Trim the seam allowance down to ⅛".

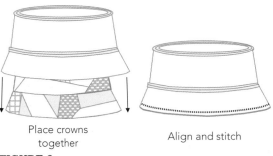

Place crowns together

Align and stitch

FIGURE 9

11 Turn the hat right side out through the opening in the lining. Whipstitch (see chapter 1) the opening closed. Tuck the lining into the outer hat. Work the lower brim between your fingers to fully roll out the seam. Press.

Unicorn Hat (with Narwhal Option)

UNICORN HAT (WITH NARWHAL OPTION)

By Melissa Averinos

The mythical, magical unicorn and its real-life marine counterpart, the narwhal, are the inspiration for these soft fleece hats. They are great for creative play or just as unique out-and-about head coverings. Simple hand stitching (beginner's fear not: instructions are included in the pattern's steps) lends artistic appeal to these gentle creatures. The unicorn hat has a flowing mane and cute little ears, while the narwhal hat has a flippy tail. Both of these hats sport an elegant horn that stands perfectly upright when the hat is worn, but is still soft, light, and flexible.

Sizes: XS–L (Toddler–Adult)

Skill Level: Beginner/Intermediate

Materials

- ½ yard fleece for the main hat. If making the horn and/or mane in a different color, purchase an additional ¼ yard in that color. For the unicorn, the designer used all white, but you can substitute with other "magical" colors. For the narwhal option, the designer used a bluish-gray for the main hat and white for the horn.
- 1 skein of pearl (sometimes spelled *perle*) cotton embroidery floss in a color that will stand out against the fleece
- Hot iron transfer pencil (available at most craft-supply stores)
- Tapestry needle
- Hot glue gun and glue sticks

NOTE: The following instructions are for the construction of a unicorn hat. Narwhal modifications are provided below each step (or group of steps).

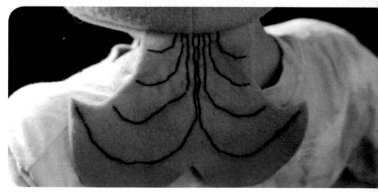

Cut the Pattern Pieces

From fleece: Cut 2 pieces of the main hat pattern from fleece. Cut 2 ear pieces from the same color as the main hat fleece. Cut 2 mirror-image pieces of each of the 3 mane pieces, using the same or a contrasting color. Cut 1 piece each of the horn core and horn spiral pieces using the same color or a contrasting color.

Narwhal Modifications: Cut 2 pieces of the main hat pattern from fleece. Cut 1 tail piece from the same fabric as the main hat. Cut 1 each of the horn core and horn spiral pieces using the contrasting fabric. Omit the ear and mane pieces.

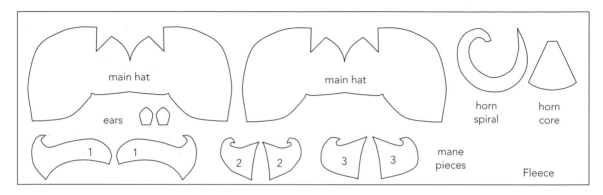

Unicorn Cutting Layout

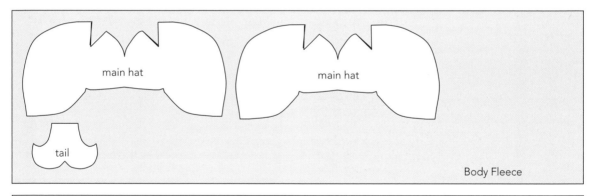

Narwhal Option Cutting Layout

FIGURE 1

Embroider the Hat
Mark the Embroidery Lines

1 Draw over the thick markings on the pattern pieces with the transfer pencil. This includes 1 main hat piece, 1 each of the 3 mane pieces, and the horn spiral. Iron the markings onto the *right side* of the fleece according to the pencil manufacturer's instructions.

Narwhal Modifications: Transfer markings to 1 main hat piece, but transfer the mouth marking instead of the nose marking. Also, transfer markings onto the horn spiral and tail pieces.

Stitch the Pieces

2 Three basic embroidery stitches are used on this hat. (Refer to Figure 2 for instructions on how to make these stitches.) All stitches are made with a tapestry needle, using the full thickness of the floss (in other words, do not untwist to separate the strands). Embroider the pieces as follows:

a. Face: Outline the eyes with a backstitch, and fill the irises with a satin stitch. Stitch the nose with a backstitch.

b. Horn Spiral: Stitch over the length of the markings with a backstitch.

c. Mane: Pin both layers of each piece together. **For *each* marking, you will make a Holbein stitch as follows:** Starting at the inner edge of the piece (the one that will be attached to the hat), make a long running stitch. When you reach the end of the marking, go back over the marking with a second running stitch to fill in the gaps.

Narwhal Modifications: Stitch the mouth, rather than the nose, with a backstitch. Stitch the single-layered tail as described for the double-layered mane (above) using the Holbein stitch.

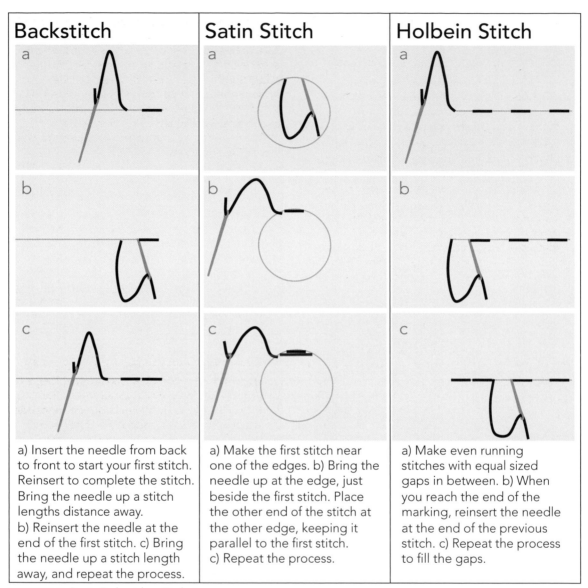

Backstitch	Satin Stitch	Holbein Stitch
a	a	a
b	b	b
c	c	c
a) Insert the needle from back to front to start your first stitch. Reinsert to complete the stitch. Bring the needle up a stitch lengths distance away. b) Reinsert the needle at the end of the first stitch. c) Bring the needle up a stitch length away, and repeat the process.	a) Make the first stitch near one of the edges. b) Bring the needle up at the edge, just beside the first stitch. Place the other end of the stitch at the other edge, keeping it parallel to the first stitch. c) Repeat the process.	a) Make even running stitches with equal sized gaps in between. b) When you reach the end of the marking, reinsert the needle at the end of the previous stitch. c) Repeat the process to fill the gaps.

FIGURE 2: Basic Embroidery Techniques

Assemble the Hat

NOTE: If you are making the narwhal, read the "Narwhal Modifications" instructions under step 5 before you proceed to step 3.

3 Fold the ear over ¼" on the left-hand side. Pin to secure. Lay out the **outer (embroidered) main hat** piece with the right side facing up. Place the bottom edge of the ear on the top edge of the left-hand dart. The folded edge should be in line with the point in the dart. Stitch into place, ⅛" from the aligned edges. Repeat on the other side, but with a mirror-image fold. **For each dart:** With the right sides facing, bring the dart edges together. Stitch ¼" from the aligned edges. (See Figure 3.)

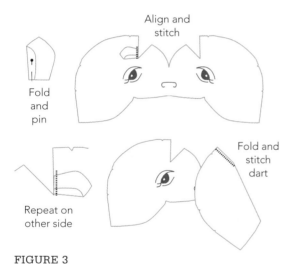

Align and stitch

Fold and pin

Repeat on other side

Fold and stitch dart

FIGURE 3

4 Apply a line of hot glue about ¼" from one of the side edges of the horn core (because the core will be covered, either side is fine). Fold the edge over ¼" and let cool. Roll the top (smaller edge) tightly and secure with a dab of glue. Arrange the bottom edge so that it is folded into thirds with the glued edge inside and the raw edge at one side. The folded core will measure about 1¾" at the bottom. Lightly glue the raw edge into place. (See Figure 4.)

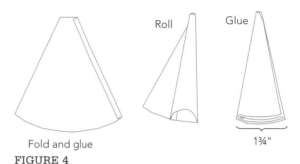

Roll

Glue

Fold and glue

1¾"

FIGURE 4

5 Lay the rolled-up horn core against the right side of the main hat piece with one folded side of the horn just in front of the dart seam. The bottom edge of the horn should overhang the top edge of the main hat by about ¼". Stitch into place, ⅛" from the top edge of the main hat. Match the notched edge of mane piece 1 with the right-hand top edge of the hat. Pin into place. Repeat with mane piece 2, which will overlap piece 1. Add mane piece 3, which will overlap piece 2, then stitch all of the mane pieces into place, ⅛" from the aligned edges. Fold the main hat piece in half and align the top/back edges with the mane and horn sandwiched in between. Stitch ¼" from the aligned edges. (See Figure 5.)

Add horn

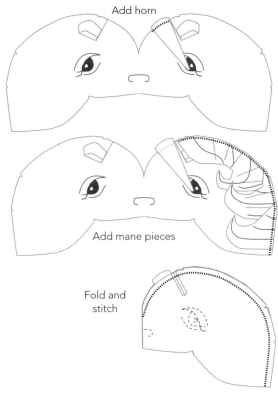

Add mane pieces

Fold and
stitch

FIGURE 5

Narwhal Modifications: Omit adding ears in step 3, but sew the darts as described. Construct the horn core as described in step 4. For step 5, position the horn at the front of the top edge. (See Figure 6.) Fold and stitch the top/back edge as described for the unicorn.

FIGURE 6

6 Turn the outer hat so the right side is facing out. Apply a small dab of glue just behind the horn core. Place the blunt end of the horn spiral on the glue with the unstitched edge touching the core. Glue the spiral around the core so that the outer edge is about ½" from the base of the core. Once you cover the blunt end, begin overlapping the inner edges with the outer edges. Use the stitching as a guide for a perfect ¼" overlap. Work in small sections, lightly gluing as you go. When you reach the top of the core, continue gluing the spiral to itself with a progressively smaller overlap, with the goal of making a tight point at the end. (See Figure 7.) **NOTE:** If you can't get the small tip to overlap nicely, simply snip the last bit away.

Narwhal Modifications: None.

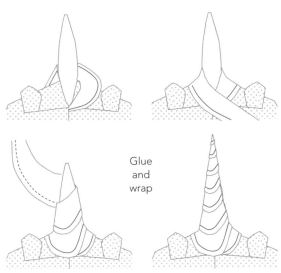

Glue
and
wrap

FIGURE 7

7 Make the darts as described in step 3 for the **inner main hat.** Bring the back/top edges together, right sides facing in. Stitch ¼" from the aligned edges, but leave the space between the two back notches open for turning. Place the inner hat over the outer hat, right sides facing. Align the bottom edges, making sure the mane and horn parts are well out of the way. Pin. Stitch the layers together, ¼" from the aligned bottom edges. (See Figure 8.)

8 Turn the hat right side out. Whipstitch (see chapter 1) the opening closed. Tuck the inner hat into the outer hat, and arrange so the seam is at the bottom edge.

Narwhal Modifications: Make the inner hat as described in step 7. With the right sides facing, center the tail over the back seam of the outer hat and align the straight edges. Stitch into place, ⅛" from the aligned edges. (See Figure 9.) Proceed with step 8.

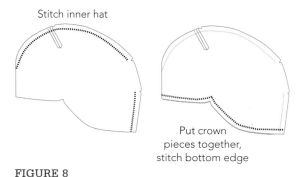

Stitch inner hat

Put crown pieces together, stitch bottom edge

FIGURE 8

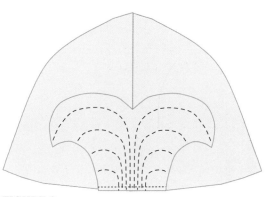

FIGURE 9

Party Hat

PARTY HAT

By Jaime Morrison Curtis and Jacinda Boneau (Prudent Baby)

This boutique-style party hat is so fun and easy to make. It features a foam core that is soft, yet durable. A simple hat trimmed with rickrack and a pom-pom at the top is great for boys and girls alike. To make a hat fit for a princess, use girlie colors and soft feather boas. Novelty prints are the perfect choice for theme parties, or you can just use bright, happy colors for years of celebrations. These hats aren't just for kids either. Go decadent with sparkly satins and lush trims for New Year's Eve or stick to basic black for an over-the-hill party. This hat is perfect for personalization with appliqué or embroidery to make for a special occasion topper.

Sizes: One size fits all

NOTE: This hat features ties or an elastic neckband. Small children should be supervised when wearing this hat.

Skill Level: Beginner

Materials

- ¼ yard lightweight woven fabric
- ½ yard heavyweight fusible interfacing (see chapter 1)
- 12" × 18" sheet of 2mm craft foam (also called *fun foam*)
- 1 yard of ¼"- to ½"-wide ribbon **or** ½ yard of ¼"-wide elastic
- EMBELLISHMENTS: Rickrack (½ yard) and a large pom-pom **or** a feather boa (at least 22")
- Hot glue gun and glue sticks

Cut the Pattern Pieces

From the fabric: Cut 2 pieces from the main hat pattern.

From the interfacing: Cut 2 pieces from the main hat pattern.

From the craft foam: Cut 1 piece from the foam insert pattern.

Elastic *or* ribbon: Cut a 16" length of elastic *or* cut two 18" pieces of ribbon.

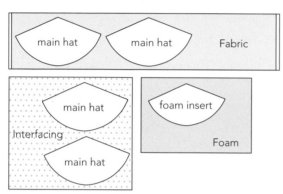

FIGURE 1: Cutting Layout

Assemble the Hat

1 Fuse the interfacing to the wrong side of the fabric pieces according to the manufacturer's instructions.

2 OPTIONAL: Sew the rickrack to the right side of the fabric piece that will be on the outside of the finished hat, 1½" from the curved bottom edge. (See Figure 2.)

Add rickrack

FIGURE 2

3 Add the fastener according to one of the instruction sets below (see Figure 3):

a. **Ribbon ties**—*For each tie:* Place one end of the tie on the right side of one of the main fabric pieces at the position indicated on the pattern. There should be about a ½" overhang at the bottom curved edge. Stitch into place, ⅛" from the edge.

b. **Elastic**—Place one end of the elastic on the right side of one of the fabric pieces at the position indicated on the pattern. There should be about a ½" overhang at the bottom curved edge. Stitch into place, ⅛" from the edge. Bring the other end over to the attachment position on the other side. Make sure you do not introduce any twists. Stitch into place, ⅛" from the edge.

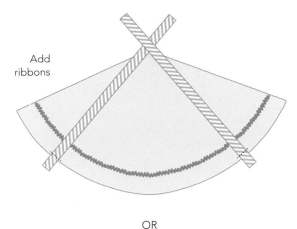

Add
ribbons

OR

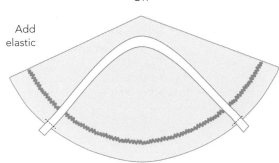

Add
elastic

FIGURE 3

4 Place the 2 main hat pieces together, right sides facing. Stitch together, ¼" from the bottom curved edges. (See Figure 4.)

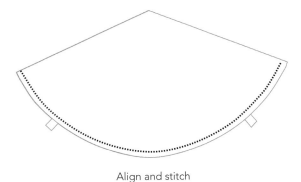

Align and stitch

FIGURE 4

5 Pull the layers apart and arrange the assembly so that it is as flat as possible and the back edges are in line. Finger press the seam allowance down against the outer hat. Starting at the tip of the outer hat, stitch ½" from the aligned edges. Stitch about 1" beyond the seam, then stop and backstitch. Make a short line of stitching (about 1" long) at the tip of the inner hat, ½" from the aligned edges. (See Figure 5.)

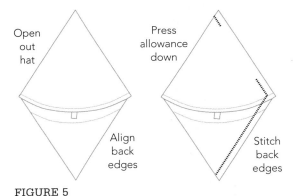

Open
out
hat

Align
back
edges

Press
allowance
down

Stitch
back
edges

FIGURE 5

6 Turn the hat right side out through the opening in the inner hat. Use a straight pin to pick out the tip, if needed. Fold the foam insert in half and insert it, tip end first, into the opening. Arrange the insert so that the back edges are positioned at the seam and the curved edges are in line with the bottom seam of the hat. Arrange the opening edges so that they are folded over ½" to the wrong side and flush with the seam allowance. Flatten out the inner hat so there is a fold at the back seam and the opening folds are in line. Stitch the opening closed, ⅛" from the aligned edges. (See Figure 6.)

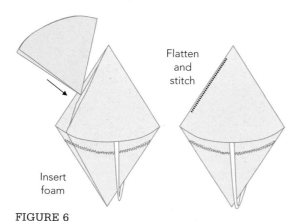

FIGURE 6

7 Insert the inner hat into the outer hat, and arrange the seam so that it is at the bottom edge of the insert. (See Figure 7.)

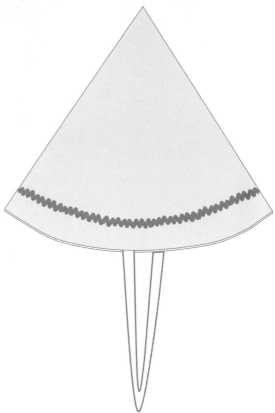

FIGURE 7

8 OPTIONAL: If you are adding a pom-pom to the tip, hot glue it into place. If you are embellishing with a feather boa, cut it to a 17" length and glue it into place at the bottom edge. To make a boa "pom-pom" for the tip, tie a knot in the boa and cut about ½" from each side of the knot. Glue it to the tip of the hat, then trim the feathers/fluff to get the desired ball shape.

Gypsy Bandana

GYPSY BANDANA

By Val Pillow & Anne Maxfield (Pillow & Maxfield)

This darling bandana is a great accessory for creative play or everyday cuteness. For gypsy dress-up, grab your tambourine and go wild by using fun trims and mock earrings. Or, you can tone it down a bit and simply mix and match your favorite prints to make a sweet kerchief. For the little guys, leave off the ruffle and trim, and sew on a single earring for quick and easy pirate play.

Sizes: XS–M (Toddler–Youth)

Skill Level: Beginner

Materials

- **Fabric:** 3 coordinating light- to mediumweight woven cotton prints (the designer used fabrics from Pillow & Maxfield's Gypsy Bandana Collection):
  * *Main bandana:* 1 fat quarter (18" × 22") or ½ yard from bolt
  * *Ties:* 1 fat quarter or ¼ yard from bolt
  * *Ruffle:* ⅛ yard from bolt
- **Pom-pom fringed trim *or* tassel-fringed trim:** ½ yard
- OPTIONAL: Gold rings (you can find with purse and belt-making supplies at most craft-supply stores)

Cut the Pattern Pieces

From main (bandana) fabric: Cut 1 piece (on a fold) from the main bandana pattern. **NOTE:** You should cut the main bandana piece on the bias, so make the fold at a 45-degree angle relative to the selvage edge.

From the tie fabric: Cut 2 pieces (on folds) from the tie pattern.

From the ruffle fabric: Cut a 3" × 43" strip.

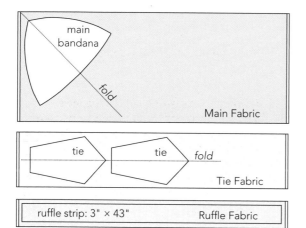

FIGURE 1: Cutting Layout

Assemble the Hat

1 Turn all 3 edges of the main bandana over ¼" to the wrong side and press. Repeat the folding and pressing process, then stitch the folds into place, ⅛" from the edges. (See Figure 2.)

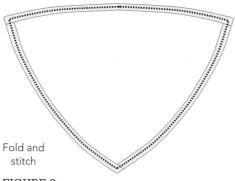

Fold and stitch

FIGURE 2

2 Zigzag or serger finish one long edge of the ruffle strip. Turn the remaining three edges of the strip over ¼" to the wrong side and press. Repeat the folding and pressing process, then stitch the folds into place, ⅛" from the edges. Run a basting stitch ¼" from the zigzag or serger finished edge. Pull the loose bobbin thread (on the underside) to gather the ruffle strip to approximately half the original length. (See Figure 3.)

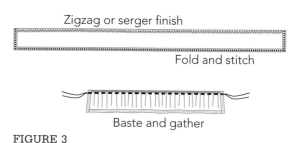

Zigzag or serger finish

Fold and stitch

Baste and gather

FIGURE 3

3 With the right sides facing, align the zigzag or serger finished edge of the ruffle with the side edges of the main bandana. Pin the ends of the ruffle into place at the sides, 1" from the front edge of the main bandana. Evenly distribute the ruffles, then stitch into place, ¼" from the aligned edges. (See Figure 4.) Pull the ruffle away from the main bandana and press the seam.

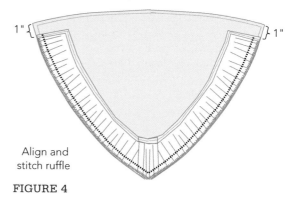

Align and stitch ruffle

FIGURE 4

4 Cut a length of trim that is 1" longer than the front edge of the main bandana. Center the trim on the wrong side of the front edge with the fringe overhanging. Pin into place. Turn the fringe under at the ends so that it is flush with the side edges (trim away excess pom-poms/tassels, if needed). Stitch into place, ⅛" from the folded front edge. Run a second line of stitching ¼" from the folded front edge. (See Figure 5.)

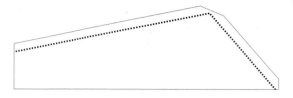

Fold, stitch, and trim

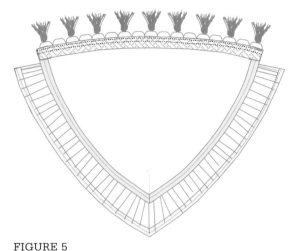

FIGURE 5

Turn, press, fold, and stitch

FIGURE 6

6 Working on the wrong side of the main bandana, center the end of one tie between the front edge and the end of the ruffle. The end should point toward the inside of the bandana, overhanging the fold by about ⅛". Stitch the tie into place by sewing back and forth, ¼" from the outer edge of the bandana. (See Figure 7.) *Repeat for the other tie.*

5 **For each tie:** Fold the tie in half lengthwise, right sides facing in. Stitch ¼" from the slanted side and bottom edges. Trim the seam allowance at the points. Turn the tie right side out through the open end and press. Fold the tie into thirds (to do this, make an "s" shape, then flatten) and zigzag or serger finish to set the fold and finish the edges. (See Figure 6.)

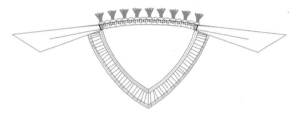

Attach ties

FIGURE 7

7 **OPTIONAL:** Attach the gold rings (to look like earrings). If the recipient is available, try the bandana on him or her and tie at the neckline. Mark the position nearest the earlobes for earring attachment. Otherwise, mark 1" from each end of the front edge. Hand sew the rings to the trim by looping thread around multiple times and tying off tightly.

Appendix: Embellishment Instructions

Embellishments are the icing on the cake when it comes to making hats! Many pre-made embellishments like patches, brooches, and bows can be purchased and attached to a finished hat. Silk flowers, buttons, beads, ribbons, and trim are also easy to add. But sometimes you can have more fun and be creative by making your own embellishments! This book's pattern designers have provided directions to make some of their favorite fabric embellishments. They are all easy to make and require very little fabric. Patterns are provided for several of the embellishments (Fleece Flower Embellishment, Silk Spiderweb Rose, and the Fabric Yo-Yos), and simple cutting dimensions are provided for the rest. Instructions are given for sewing the embellishments directly to the hats, but you can hot glue them into place if you prefer. To make the embellishments removable, simply glue them to a bar pin or sew onto a safety pin, and then attach them to the hat.

Bows

FABRIC BOW
By Anneliese S.

To make the fabric bow used in the Fantastic Fedora, cut rectangles to the dimensions specified in the table for the desired bow size. (*NOTE: An inner piece, cut from canvas, provides structure to the bow, but you can omit it if you are working with a thicker fabric or just prefer a softer bow.*) Place the fashion fabric main bow pieces together, right sides facing. Place the canvas main bow piece atop the stack, if applicable. Align the edges. Stitch the layers together, ¼" from the edges, leaving a 1" opening in the center of one of the long edges. Snip the seam allowance at the corners. Turn right side out, and pick the corners out with the tip of a straight pin. Sew the opening closed with a hand needle and thread. (See Figure 1.)

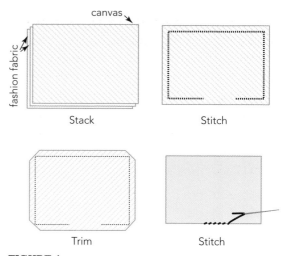

Stack   Stitch

Trim   Stitch

FIGURE 1

Place the center tie pieces together, right sides facing. Stitch together, ¼" from the edges, leaving one short end open. Trim the seam allowance at the corners. Turn the center tie right side out, then fold the raw edge over about ⅛" to one side, and hand stitch into

Finished Bow Size	Main Bow (*cut 2 of outer fabric, cut 1 of inner canvas*)	Center Tie (*cut 2 of outer fabric*)
Small (3½" wide)	4 × 3"	1¼ × 2½"
Medium (5" wide)	5½ × 3¼"	1½ × 2¾"
Large (5½" wide)	6 × 3½"	1¾ × 3"

TABLE: Dimensions of Bow Components

place. Form a loop with the center piece, over-lapping the ends by about ¼". Make sure the raw end is on the *inside* of the loop and hand stitch into place. Slip the main bow through the loop and arrange it so that it is centered and the hand stitching is in the middle of the loop on the back side. Make a few stitches on the back of the bow to secure the loop to the center. (See Figure 2.) Sew into place on the hat.

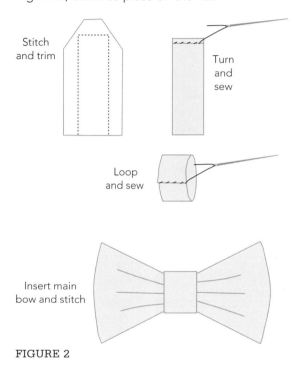

FIGURE 2

FLAT RIBBON BOW
By Dolin O'Shea

To make the bow as shown on the Jackie Pillbox Hat, you will need ¾ yard of 1½"-wide grosgrain ribbon. **NOTE:** The finished bow is 11" long tip-to-tip and has loops that are half as long as the ends, but you can modify the ribbon length and/or the loop stitching position to get a different look. This folding and stitching technique can also be used with different widths of ribbons to get smaller or larger bows.

Cut a 22" length of ribbon. Fold the ribbon in half widthwise, wrong side facing in (if applicable) and press to make a crease. Stitch 5½" from the fold. Arrange the loop so that the crease is centered over the seam. Stitch into place at the crease. (See Figure 1.)

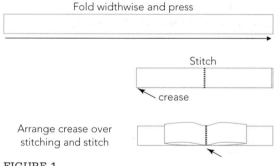

FIGURE 1

Fold the entire piece in half lengthwise, loop sides facing in. Run a short line (no more than ¾" long) of stitching at the center, ¼" from the folded edge. Unfold. You'll see that this stitching makes a small pleat on the loop side of the folded ribbon. (See Figure 2.)

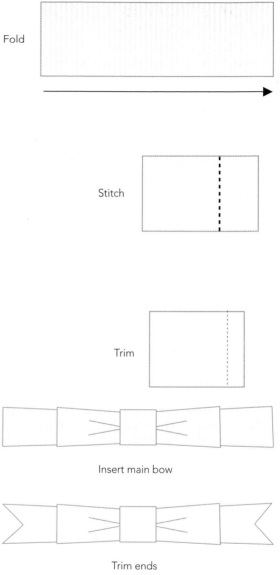

Fold

Stitch

Trim

Insert main bow

Trim ends

FIGURE 3

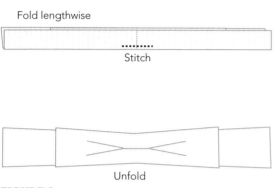

Fold lengthwise

Stitch

Unfold

FIGURE 2

Cut a 3" length of ribbon. Fold in half widthwise, wrong side facing in (if applicable). Stitch 1" from the folded edge. Trim the raw ends, leaving about ¼" seam allowance. This forms a small loop. Slip the main bow through the loop and arrange it so that it is centered and the raw edges are in the middle of the loop on the back side. Make a few stitches on the back of the bow to secure the loop to the center. Clip the ends into a "V" shape, if desired, and heat seal or apply a liquid seam sealant (such as Fray Check™) to the ends. (See Figure 3.) Sew into place on the hat.

Fabric Yo-Yos
By Scott and Linda Hansen

To make the fabric yo-yo mentioned in the Andrea/Andrew Hat pattern, cut out a circle using the Fabric Yo-Yo pattern piece labeled with the desired finished size. Thread a hand needle with a 36" length of strong thread that is held double. Tie the thread in a knot at the end. Start folding the edges of the fabric circle over ¼" to the wrong side, securing with long running stitches as you go. Fold and stitch all the way around the circle. (See Figure 1.)

Pull the thread to draw the circle into a pouch shape with the right side facing out. Flatten out so that the opening is in the center. (See Figure 2.) Secure with a few stitches. Add a decorative button or bead to the center, if desired. Sew into place on the hat.

Gather and flatten

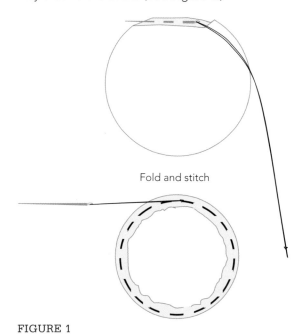

Fold and stitch

FIGURE 1

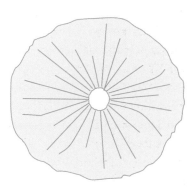

FIGURE 2

Fleece Pom-Pom
By Jennifer Hagedorn

To create a fleece pom-pom for the Stocking Cap or Fleece Beanie pattern, cut a 12" × 3" strip of fleece. Fold in half lengthwise. Snip along the aligned long raw edges about every ¼"–½", leaving the last ⅛" from the fold uncut. Unfold the strip. (See Figure 1.)

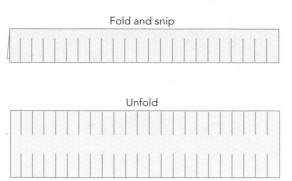

Fold and snip

Unfold

FIGURE 1

Roll the strip widthwise, right side facing out. Thread a hand needle with a 36" length of strong thread that is held double. Tie the thread in a knot at the end. Push the needle through the center of the pom-pom (you may need a thimble to help you). Wrap the thread tightly around the center a few times. Bring the needle

back through the center again, then tie a knot. Stitch the pom-pom into place at the top of the hat. (See Figure 2.) Fluff and trim as needed.

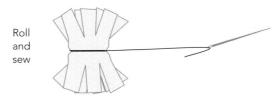

Roll and sew

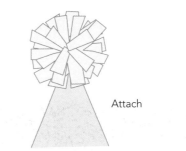

Attach

FIGURE 2

Flowers

FLEECE FLOWER
By Jennifer Hagedorn

To make a fleece flower for the Fleece Beanie pattern, cut 5 circles of fleece or felt using the Fleece Flower Embellishment pattern piece in the desired size (the finished flower will come out the same size as the starting circles). (**OPTIONAL:** Cut 5 circles from tulle and place 1 circle on the wrong side of each fleece circle before folding.) Fold each circle in half, wrong sides together. Place one folded circle on top of another with the centers in line and perpendicular to one another. Add a third circle that is centered with the first two, and the folded edge in line with the first circle's edge. Add the fourth circle to complete the circular arrangement. Stick the top of this circle under the first circle. The arrangement should look like the top of a cardboard box with overlapped flaps. (See Figure 1.)

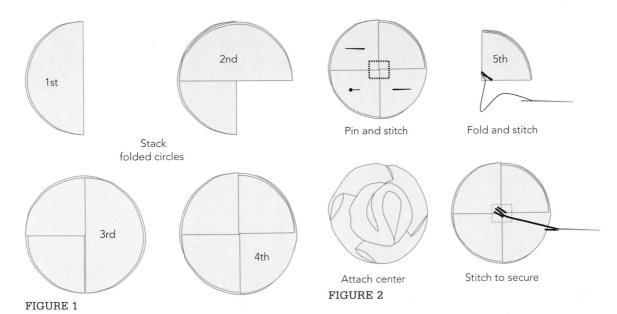

FIGURE 1

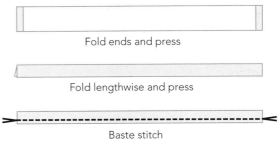

FIGURE 2

Pin the flower together, then sew in a box shape in the center to secure the middle of the flower base. Fold the remaining circle in half again, so it is now folded in quarters. Thread a hand needle with a 36" length of strong thread that is held doubled. Tie the thread in a knot at the end. Make a few small stitches near the point of the fifth piece, catching all the layers. Feed the needle through the center of the flower base, nesting the fifth folded circle in the center. Make a few more small stitches to secure the center to the flower base, then tie a knot. (See Figure 2.) Stitch the flower into place on the hat.

GATHERED FABRIC ROSETTE
By Shelly Figueroa

To make a rosette for the Turn It Up Hat, cut a 3" × 32" strip of fabric. (**NOTE:** You can cut the strip on the bias for a fluffier flower, but ¾ yard of fabric is required.) Fold the short ends over ½" to the wrong side and press. Fold the strip in half lengthwise, wrong side facing in, and press. Run a row of basting stitches ¼" from the aligned raw edges. (See Figure 1.)

Fold ends and press

Fold lengthwise and press

Baste stitch

FIGURE 1

Pull the bobbin threads to gather. Roll the gathered edge to form the base of the rosette. Use a hand needle and thread to sew the layers together near the base as you go. Tie a knot, then sew into place on the hat. (See Figure 2.) Fluff the finished rosette.

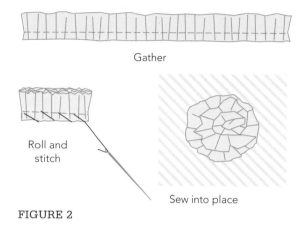

Gather

Roll and stitch

Sew into place

FIGURE 2

SILK SPIDERWEB ROSE
By Lisa Carroccio

This silk spiderweb rose looks terrific on the Liesl Cloche. For this project, you will need ¼ yard silk shantung or dupioni, matching embroidery floss, embroidery needle, small (4–5" diameter) embroidery hoop, large safety pin, and a decorative button (optional). Cut a square and a strip to the dimensions listed in the table for the desired rose size. (**NOTE:** To give more character to the rose, create the strip by snipping and tearing rather than cutting, which will fray the edges.) With a washable marker or pencil, trace or transfer the appropriate sized stitching guide from the Silk Spiderweb Rose pattern piece to the center of the square. Thread the embroidery needle with a full thickness (all the strands, not unwound) of floss. Insert the needle through the backside of the square at point a. Reinsert at point b, making a loose stitch that droops down to the center point. Stick the needle through the back of the fabric at the center point, *catching* the previous stitch. Reinsert the needle at point c. Make the final stitch from point d to point e, passing the needle under the stitch that attaches to point b. This will give you a five-spoked wheel. (See Figure 1.)

Finished Rose Size	Strip	Foundation Square
Small (2½" wide)	1" × 40"	6" × 6"
Medium (3" wide)	1½" × 40"	
Large (3½" wide)	2" × 40"	

TABLE: Silk Spiderweb Rose Components

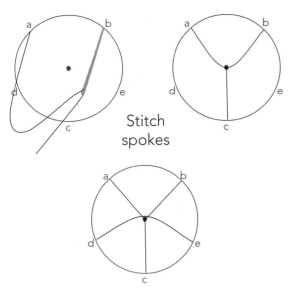

Stitch
spokes

FIGURE 1

Tie a knot in the back of the fabric, but do not cut the thread just yet. Sew one end of the fabric strip into place at the center point of the "spoked wheel." Attach a safety pin to the other end of your fabric strip. Use the pin to weave the strip over and under the spokes in a circular fashion. (See Figure 2.)

Twist the strip as you create your rose. Once you have covered all of your spokes, remove the safety pin and tuck the end under the rose. Using the needle and thread that is still attached to the back of the fabric, secure the rose with a few stitches. (See Figure 3.) Cut out your finished rose, making sure to not cut your foundation spokes. Sew into place on the hat.

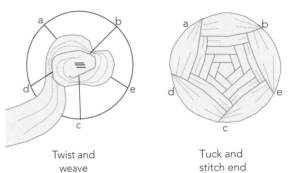

Twist and
weave

Tuck and
stitch end

FIGURE 3

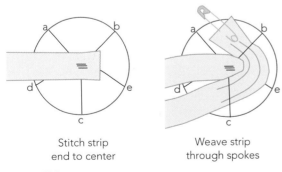

Stitch strip
end to center

Weave strip
through spokes

FIGURE 2

Contributing Designers

Alexia Abegg   Alexia Marcelle Abegg began sewing as a young girl, inspired by her mother's sewing and *Sassy* magazine. From quilting to accessories and clothing, she loves to sew it all! Studying Fine Arts and Fashion Design in college, and a stint in NYC, gave her the inspiration to pursue art quilting and sewing pattern design. She can't be away from the sewing machine for more than a day. You can find out more about Alexia at http://www.greenbeepatterns.com/.

Mary Abreu   After stitching her first pillow by hand at age eight, author Mary Abreu received a Holly Hobbie sewing machine, which she quickly ignored because the toy machine only sewed a chain stitch. Mary documents her many crafting adventures on her blog, Confessions of a Craft Addict (www.confessionsofacraftaddict.com), because her family grew tired of the daily craft show-and-tell. She teaches sewing classes in Atlanta, GA, and enjoys sewing Neo-Victorian creations for herself—when she can tear herself away from sewing her daughter's wardrobe. When not sewing, she enjoys photography, baking, and beating her husband and teenage sons at Scrabble®.

Bari J. Ackerman   The designer behind the Bari J. brand is Bari J. Ackerman. The brand debuted in 2004 featuring handbags and accessories. In 2009, Bari changed the focus of the business to fabric and surface design and sewing patterns. Her first book, *Inspired to Sew,* was published in 2011. Today, along with limited-edition handbags and accessories, she has a line of "Keeping It Real" sewing patterns.

Melissa Averinos Melissa Averinos is a fabric designer, painter, good listener, and lover of strawberry rhubarb pie. Melissa currently designs for Andover Fabrics. She wrote *Small Stash Sewing: 24 Projects Using Designer Fat Quarters* (Wiley, 2010). For inspiration and juicy honesty, visit Melissa at her blog: www.yummygoods.com.

Jacinda Boneau Jacinda Boneau is co-founder of Prudent Baby, the premier destination for crafty moms seeking ways to make their lives even more stylish and beautiful. PrudentBaby.com provides sewing and crafting tutorials, recipes, party themes, and home decorating inspiration. Jacinda is also currently developing her first fabric collection.

Lisa Carroccio Lisa Carroccio's blog may be called The Domestic Diva's Disaster™ (http://thedomesticdiva.wordpress.com/), but the lifelong New Yorker has inspired thousands with her sewing tutorials, kids' clothing designs, and sewing room organization series. Lisa built a successful eBay® children's custom clothing business, then turned her attention to manufacturing and launched Downtown Joey at http://downtownjoey.com (named for her son), which offers a line of casual contemporary clothing for boys. Although her focus is on boys' clothing, Lisa can still be found sewing yards of silk shantung and tulle to create one-of-a-kind special occasion girls' dresses. She also campaigns for organ donation awareness because her own daughter is a two-time transplant patient.

Jess Christian   Jess Christian runs a blog called Craftiness is not Optional (http://www.craftinessisnotoptional.com/), where she discusses her love of sewing and all things crafty! She has two adorable daughters, Sadie and Charlotte, and an awesome hubby who patiently supports her crafting/sewing impulses. Jess especially enjoys sewing children's clothing and hoarding fabric. She's mostly self-taught and loves to figure out how things are made.

Kim Christopherson   Kim Christopherson is the founder of www. YouCanMakeThis.com and www.SWAKembroidery.com. She is also the owner of Kimberbell Designs, specializing in sewing, quilt, and embroidery patterns. In 2010, Kim and her identical twin sister, Kris, began hosting the popular online show, "The DIY Dish" (www.theDIYdish.com). Their weekly show features craft and fabric-related projects for home decor, accessories, quilts, embroidery, and more. Kim has been featured in magazines and on local and national television shows including *The Rachael Ray Show* and *The Nate Berkus Show*. Between juggling children's schedules with soccer, music lessons, and homework, she enjoys sewing with friends and photography.

Jaime Morrison Curtis   Jaime Morrison Curtis is co-founder of *Prudent Baby*, Los Angeles Editor for *DailyCandy Kids*, editor at *Babble Family Style*, and author of the award-winning book *Prudent Advice: Lessons for My Baby Daughter (A Life List for Every Woman)* (Andrews McMeel, 2010), which hit a nerve with mothers, grandmothers, and daughters around the world with its unique voice and updated take on age-old wisdom passed down from generation to generation. She lives in Los Angeles where she enjoys sewing, cooking (not baking), and champagne.

Joanna Figueroa   Joanna Figueroa is a licensed designer for MODA fabrics, beloved for her numerous fabric collections in her signature Fresh Vintage™ style. Joanna also co-owns and operates Fig Tree & Company along with her husband Eric. Fig Tree & Co. specializes in a fresh take on traditional quilting and sewing patterns, and currently offers more than 150 stand-alone patterns and booklets. She has written several books, including her newest title, *With Fabric & Thread*. Her work is regularly featured in industry publications such as *American Patchwork & Quilting®*, *Quilts & More®*, *American Quilt Retailer*, *Quiltmania*, and *Where Women Create*. Find out more about Joanna on her blog figtreequilts.typepad.com or through her website, www.figtreeandcompany.com.

Shelly Figueroa   Shelly Figueroa is the founder of Figgy's, (www.figgyspatterns.com) a sewing pattern company offering simple, modern, and contemporary patterns for children. She is a member of the Portland Modern Quilt guild. She is a sewing instructor for Modern Domestic Sewing Studio and is well known at the local fabric shops in Portland, Oregon, for workshops and pattern design. Shelley has been featured on the pages of *Sewing World*, *Sew Hip*, *Sew WOW*, *Craftzine*, *Making*, *Cloth*, and *Simply Homemade* magazines and on numerous sewing/crafting blogs around the world. She currently resides in Portland, Oregon, with her husband, Adam, and two sons. You can find Shelley on Twitter at @figgys.

Jennifer Hagedorn   Jen Hagedorn is the pattern-making diva behind Tie Dye Diva patterns (http://www.tiedyedivapatterns.com/). She began her online business creating hand-dyed clothing and play silks, and retained the Tie Dye Diva name for her line of sewing patterns that launched in 2007. Her favorite designs are those that include a touch of whimsy, like ruffled-bottom babywear or tiny hats with a great big flower. Besides sewing and fabric shopping, Jen's great loves include her husband and three kids, chili-infused chocolate, and collecting sea glass.

Linda & Scott Hansen   Linda Hansen is a self-taught mixed media artist. She is primarily an art doll artist, which is perfect because her favorite mediums to play with are paper clay, fabric, fibers, and beads. Linda has been published in *Art Doll Quarterly™*, *Somerset Studio™*, *Soft Dolls and Animals!*, Teesha Moore's zine *Art and Play*, *Doll Crafter and Costuming*, and in the book *Art Doll Adventures*. Recently, Linda has been doing costume design with her daughter. Linda's website is www.missmabelstudio.com. Scott Hansen is also self-taught in his art form: quilting. Scott runs Blue Nickel Studios, his quilt design business, out of his home. He is on staff at *Generation Q*, a modern magazine about quilting, sewing, and all things related to needles, fabric, and thread. His quilt designs have been featured in various quilt magazines and he is working on a book featuring his own quilt patterns. Scott merges a mix of modern and traditional influences and is inpired by the things he sees around the cityscape of Seattle and its environs. Scott's website is www.bluenickelstudios.com.

Karen LePage   Karen LePage runs, crafts, and writes. She's a gentle-living, hard-rocking, granola-geek-like, yoga-practicing, veggie-eating, wife-mom-friend-sister-daughter-artist. When not chasing her young daughter or debating with her teenage son, she co-hosts a monthly craft meet-up, designs sewing patterns, teaches sewing classes, volunteers in local craft communities, and makes handsewn kid's clothes. She sells custom children's clothing in her etsy shop (http://onegirlcircus.etsy.com/) and writes a sewing advice column for the *Handmade Companion* (launching in 2012!). Karen runs a website resource to support *Sewing for Boys*, a book she co-wrote with Shelly Figueroa at http://sewing-for-boys.com/. And Karen sporadically blogs at http://onegirlcircus.com/.

Kathy Mack   Kathy Mack lives on Bainbridge Island, Washington, with her two teenage daughters and a husband who supports all her wacky ideas. Her grandmother taught her to sew as a little girl and she loves it as much today as she did after taking that first stitch. Kathy spends her days as the proprietress of Pink Chalk Fabrics, an online fabric shop for modern sewists. She writes about her creative work and inspiration at http://PinkChalkStudio.com/blog. You'll find Kathy's line of Pink Chalk Studio sewing patterns at independent quilt and fabric shops across the United States.

Kaari Meng Kaari Meng grew up in a large, creative family in southern California. After graduating from the University of San Francisco with a degree in Political Science, Kaari headed to New York City to work for the Metropolitan Museum of Art. Once bitten by the creative bug, Kaari returned to school and studied jewelry making. After designing a line of vintage jewelry for ten years, Kaari opened French General in an old barn along the Hudson River. Eventually, Kaari moved the collection to Los Angeles, where it is located near Dodger Stadium in Silverlake. French General is a French-inspired collection of creative supplies for the artist, crafter, and collector. Kaari and her husband, JZ, also design quilting fabric and patterns for Moda as well as a paper arts line for Jolees Boutique. French General fabric, notions, and jewelry kits are available online at www.frenchgeneral.com and you can read more about Kaari's musings at www.frenchgeneral.blogspot.com.

Heather Niziolek Heather Niziolek is the owner/designer behind the Goosie Girl label. (Most people call her "Goose.") Goose values her client relationships just as much as her personal friendships. Goose is inspired by music, nature, her extended family, and by that inner whisper she hears late at night saying, "If you can dream it, you can achieve it." Each of her creations is an original design. Celebrities who own Goosie Girl products include Claudia Schiffer, Kevin Costner, Will Smith, Christina Applegate, and Halle Berry. You can find out more about Goosie Girl at http://goosiegirl boutique.com/.

Dolin O'Shea After spending fifteen years in the fashion industry as a pattern maker and technical designer, in 2008 Dolin O'Shea decided to leave the corporate world behind to pursue more creative opportunities. She has honed her couture dressmaking skills by making quite a few wedding dresses. Dolin has several published magazine articles and she was a technical writer, illustrator, and pattern maker for two books, *Girl's World* and *Happy Home*. Her next adventure is to expand her independently published line of patterns for knitting, crochet, and sewing. She lives in San Jose, California, with a wonderful husband and two silly dogs. You can learn about more about Dolin at www.lulubliss.com.

Jennifer Paganelli   Jennifer Paganelli grew up in the Virgin Islands and weaves that beauty into everything she creates. A crafter and hand sewer, she loves to create items that echo her past. Foraging through vintage finds and cast-offs stimulates her imagination and she is piqued by the hunt. Taking those finds and telling a story is where her magic comes into play. Jennifer drenches her fabric designs in sun-kissed hues and she also has a line of home furnishings. She has recently written two books, *Girls World* and *Happy Home*. She resides in Connecticut with her husband, children, and her Labradoodle, George. To find out more about Jennifer, visit http://www.sis boom.com.

Pillow & Maxfield   Val Pillow and Anne Maxfield have combined creative forces to launch their licensing design studio, Pillow & Maxfield (http://www. pillowandmaxfield.com/). The duo creates designs for products to enhance your home, inspire your creativity, and add a little panache to your personal style. With more than twenty-five years of experience in the Social Expressions Industry, they have extensive backgrounds in design and product development. Pillow & Maxfield fabrics are sold in hundreds of brick-and-mortar stores and through online shops. You can find their designs on numerous products such as baby layette collections, diaper bag collections, and personal travel accessories.

Irene Rodegerdts   Irene Rodegerdts has an active family who loves to do just about anything. She's a mother to three children: August, Edward, and Olivia. Her husband teaches science while she gets to stay home with their kids. She lives in the Northwest and enjoys the mountains, beaches, and valleys during her children's frequent school breaks. She loves just about any craft and hopes she will get more time to do them as her kids grow up . . . slowly, but surely! You can read more about Irene's crafty adventures at http://mushroomvillagers.wordpress.com/.

Anneliese of Aesthetic Nest   Anneliese is the author of the blog, Aesthetic Nest (http://www.aestheticnest.com), which is a journal of her many creative pursuits. The mother of three daughters, who are her muses, Anneliese is driven to create beauty in her daily life and to fashion memorable family celebrations. Since making Aesthetic Nest public in 2010, Anneliese's sewing, knitting, crochet, and party designs have been featured on many notable craft and design sites and earned her the "Most Beautiful Craft Blog" award in 2011. Having recently left her career in marketing to stay home full time, Anneliese has made the leap from following patterns to designing her own, which gives her yet another reason to stay up at night.

Bonnie Shaffer   Bonnie Shaffer is a milliner and makes retro-style hats for men and women. The fabulous quality of vintage fabrics really inspires her. She has a huge collection of vintage wools and buckles and is always on the hunt for more! Bonnie has an Etsy shop (http://www.bonniesknitting.etsy.com) where she sells her wares. She has collaborated with designers from around the world and creates everything from foul-mouthed puppets to leather gorgets to spats, crowns, and sword belts. Bonnie enjoys it all but absolutely *loves* making hats! You can find Bonnie on Facebook at https://www.facebook.com/Bonniesknitting.

Melissa Stramel   Melissa Stramel is a creative mother of three. While sewing for her children, she was inspired to start her business, Lilac Lane, which grew into a store in her home of Colby, Kansas, called Creations Gallery. Her inspiring ideas soon led her to create a blog and start to work on designing her own patterns. In 2010, Melissa began designing fabrics to fill a void she saw in the industry; she wanted something beautiful, yet fun which could be enjoyed by women of all ages. Her fabrics are a culmination of childhood memories and her love of flower gardening. Please visit her online at melissastramel.com. Melissa's fabrics are produced by Andover Fabrics, and her patterns are produced by QuiltWoman.com.

Betz White   Betz White has built a career on thoughtful design, skilled craftsmanship, and a focus on materials that are kind to people and planet alike. She is a designer, green crafter, and the best-selling author of two books that encourage readers to "stitch beautifully, tread lightly," *Warm Fuzzies* (North Light, 2007) and *Sewing Green* (STC Craft, 2009). Her original sewing patterns, Make New or Make Do™, are designed to be made from either new or repurposed fabrics and are sold in specialty fabric shops nationwide. As the perfect earth-friendly complement to her pattern line, Betz debuted her first coordinated collection of organic cotton sheeting with the Robert Kaufman Company in 2011. When she's not designing or sewing,

Betz can be found shopping at thrift stores, teaching workshops, and raising two crafty boys with a passion for making stuff. To learn more about her current and upcoming projects and blog, visit http://blog.betzwhite.com/.

Patty Young   Patty Young grew up in San Jose, Costa Rica, in an environ-
ment where she was encouraged to express her creativity freely. Her family
moved to the United States in 1987 and Patty attended the University of
Central Florida, where she received a degree in Graphic Design and
Photography. Currently, Patty is the co-owner and designer of MODKID, LLC,
which specializes in boutique sewing patterns for children's and women's
clothing as well as purses and home accessories. Patty is also a licensed tex-
tiles designer for New York-based Michael Miller Fabrics. Patty's first book,
Sewing MODKID Style (Wiley Publishing), was released in 2012. Her designs
and creative studio have been featured in numerous national and interna-
tional magazines and trade publications. Visit her website at http://www.modkidboutique.com/ and
keep up with all things Patty on her popular blog, http://www.modkidboutique.blogspot.com.

Index

About the Author

Carla Hegeman Crim, founder of Scientific Seamstress LLC, is a molecular biologist turned patternmaker. She has a B.S. in Biology from Virginia Commonwealth University, a Ph.D. in Plant Physiology from Virginia Tech, and was a Postdoctoral Fellow at Cornell University. She is a self-taught seamstress who has been experimenting with fabric since she was a wee little girl. When her son came along, she decided to build a home-based sewing business. For the first few years, she focused on elaborate clothing and furniture designs for collector dolls. She had many requests for her patterns and began publishing them in 2006. Scientific Seamstress patterns are known for their step-by-step instructions and detailed illustrations. In addition to her own line of patterns, she collaborates with fabric designer Jennifer Paganelli on a series of Sis Boom patterns for children and adults. When Carla isn't in her sewing lab, she enjoys gardening, yoga, and spending time with her family. Visit her blog (http://scientificseamstress.blogspot.com) for tips, tutorials, and experiments with design. Learn more about her patterns on her website (http://scientificseamstress.com).